DONALD COZZENS

FAITH
THAT DARES
TO SPEAK

LITURGICAL PRESS
Collegeville, Minnesota

www.litpress.org

Cover design by Ann Blattner.

1   2   3   4   5   6   7   8

Library of Congress Cataloging-in-Publication Data

Cozzens, Donald B.
      Faith that dares to speak / Donald Cozzens.
            p.   cm.
      Includes bibliographical references and index.
      ISBN 0-8146-3018-9 (alk. paper)
      1. Catholic Church—Government.   2. Church renewal—Catholic Church.
I. Title.

BX1803.C69   2004
282'.09'0511—dc22

                                                           2004011923

To

THEODORE M. HESBURGH, C.S.C.

PRIEST, EDUCATOR, STATESMAN

Other titles by Donald Cozzens available from Liturgical Press:

Sacred Silence: Denial and the Crisis in the Church

The Changing Face of the Priesthood: A Reflection on the Priest's Crisis of Soul

CONTENTS

ACKNOWLEDGMENTS

FOR THE PAST TWO YEARS I have taught in the religious studies department at John Carroll University in Cleveland. The welcome extended to me by the university's president, Edward Glynn, S.J., assistant to the president for mission and identity, Howard Gray, S.J., and the Jesuit community made me aware of and thankful for the grace of being at home with brothers.

I am also grateful to the dean of the College of Arts and Sciences, Nick R. Baumgartner, religious studies department chairs Paul Lauritzen and Joseph Kelly, and academic vice president David M. La Guardia for welcoming me in numerous practical ways to the John Carroll faculty. These colleagues provided the space and time to write this book. I have benefited greatly from the work of two superb graduate assistants, Lisa Wells and Eric Abercrombie, while writing *Faith That Dares to Speak*. Their competence was matched by their genuine humanity and goodness. Leslie Curtis of John Carroll's art history department deepened my appreciation of Lyonel Feininger's work, which graces the cover of this book.

I am thankful to friends who read various drafts of *Faith That Dares to Speak* and offered particularly helpful suggestions: Colette Ackerman, O.C.D., Alison Benders, John Dreese, Conrad Gromada, Mary Catherine Hilkert, O.P., and Robert Toth. Informal contributions to the concepts shaping the text were made by the Saturday morning "coffee house theologians" who have held court with vigor and humor for more than fifteen years. Throughout the writing of this book, I found encouragement and advice from friends who met with me for monthly dinners in Cleveland's Little Italy. Special thanks to Michael Tevesz for gathering these scholars and colleagues.

Finally, my enduring gratitude to my family—Mary Ann and Tom Cozzens, Pat and Jim Cozzens, Maryellen and Dan Dombek. I find in their company safe harbor, good conversation, and healing laughter.

DONALD BERNARD COZZENS

OCTAVE OF EASTER, 2004
CLEVELAND, OHIO

INTRODUCTION

LET ME SAY AT THE BEGINNING that I write to convince the reader of nothing. Convincing, I have come to understand, is the preoccupation and passion of politicians and debaters, among others. It rises up, for the most part, from ideology. Speech that rises up from faith should have a different tone, a different quality. It surfaces from the experience of a relationship—a relationship with God and others in the Spirit. Like the gospel, it should be fundamentally a witness, an invitation to ponder and consider. Nor do I write to complain or protest. I trust I have a healthy, historically grounded respect for the way things are, as well as a vision of the way things might be, *ought* to be; a vision rooted in the gospel and the Second Vatican Council. The vision, of course, is the vision of the church itself and must be claimed in story and deed; that is, held in memory (tradition) and bravely lived out in history. This book is about this task in this time.

Few question today the claim that the Catholic church in the United States—and in many other parts of our world—is in trouble. It is wrestling with the greatest crisis in its relatively short history. And in times of crisis, each believer has a responsibility to engage the crisis to the best of his or her ability. I would like to think that *Faith That Dares to Speak* is my attempt to engage the crisis.

In the pages that follow I invite you, the reader, into a passionate conversation about this beloved church of ours. Much is at stake here: the sacramental character of the church; its mission of liberation in the *way of Jesus*; the role of the laity and particularly the role of women; the future of ministry; the church's structures of governance. These and other issues are weighty and serious. They require that the church draws upon its many and varied resources not only to weather the present storm but to emerge from

3

it a healthier, humbler, more compassionate, more vibrant church. We are in this together as members of the household of God.

In the first four chapters that follow—The Courage to Speak, The Humility to Listen, Love That Dares to Question, Faith That Dares to Speak—I probe and examine the forces that make passionate, adult engagement in the church's life difficult and foreboding. They are indeed formidable as you will see. Some are internal to the believer and center around issues of identity and integrity. Others are external, rooted in the structures and systems of the institutional church.

The final four chapters—The Liberation of the Laity, The Voice of the Faithful, Contemplative Conversation, A Rising Chorus—identify the social and ecclesial factors that support my contention that things will never quite be the same. Whether or not we can overcome our tendency to fear and mistrust will determine if this new day will be a day of blessing or a day of bitter regret.

My purpose in writing this book, therefore, is to foster understanding of the task at hand and to underscore why it deserves our best energies and efforts. At first glance, *Faith That Dares to Speak* may not appear to be very practical. But I firmly believe that speaking honestly from our experiences of Christian living and discipleship is profoundly practical. I believe that listening humbly allows God's Spirit to inspire and direct us especially in moments of darkness and confusion. And I believe that expressing the questions we have about our church's structures and forms of governance are signs of fidelity rather than sounds of discontent or disloyalty. The first practical step to healthy renewal and reform guided by the Spirit is to reverence the power of speech that rises up from commitment and love. These important and oftentimes painful conversations are foundational to the life of the church. We dare not run from them in search of some temporary, but deceptive, calm. Doing so is to indulge in denial, which only makes matters worse, much worse.

As much as this book is a call to candid speech it is at the same time a call to silence. It is in silence that the grains of ego and pride are sifted out of our visions and convictions, our causes and crusades. We need at this moment a faith that dares to be silent, that dares to be still. Only in silence does the heart learn to speak words that heal and invite and instruct.

So, consider *Faith That Dares to Speak* an invitation to join the conversation. I assume only this: that the reader treasures the gospel and embraces the vision of the Second Vatican Council. Joining the conversation will not always be easy—but it is critically important. By the grace of God we are disciples of the Christ and members of God's household. It is time to come home and to speak humbly but fearlessly in the presence of our sisters and brothers.

CHAPTER ONE

THE COURAGE TO SPEAK

The courage of life is often a less dramatic spectacle than the courage of a final moment; but it is no less a magnificent mixture of triumph and tragedy. A man does what he must—in spite of personal consequences, in spite of obstacles and dangers and pressures—and that is the basis of all morality.

—John F. Kennedy

O God, give us serenity to accept what cannot be changed; courage to change what should be changed; and wisdom to distinguish the one from the other.

—Reinhold Niebuhr

WITHIN THE HEART OF EVERY COMMITTED DISCIPLE exists a storehouse of experiences and memories that determine the contours, the straight and crooked legs, of his or her journey of faith. Experienced and remembered from the vantage point of faith, these defining moments affirm the abiding presence of grace in the disciple's journey. They are, so to speak, grace-notes revealing the mostly hidden workings of God's spirit in our everyday lives. Whether they are painful memories of petty or serious betrayals, memories of unseen fidelity and compassion, or memories of graced achievement or embarrassing failures, they become the fonts of personal wisdom. To live our lives with any kind of integrity means that we carry within us the spiritual scars that inevitably mark and transform our souls as we continue the fundamental journey of faith.

In aggregate, these grace-points of communion and reconciliation give shape to our individual stories of faith. They are the confirming, lingering tastes of the divine graciousness. From time to time, it is as if faith is transcended and one no longer believes, *she knows*. Staying the course through the windstorms of life, the disciple discovers a strength and peace clearly not her own. And a joy that defies explanation.

Drawing on this storehouse of graced experiences and memories truly makes one wise with a wisdom that reaches beyond the boundaries of personal, finite existence. And it keeps one on course, keeps the disciple faithful to the gospel in good times and bad. But perhaps more importantly, the disciple *discovers that she has something to say*. She has something to say to herself—a profound expression of gratitude for the sustaining graces that have carried her to this point in her life. But the disciple also has something to say to the fellowship of disciples, to the church. This is so because believers sustain each other with their stories of grace and healing. They bear witness to the Spirit working not only in individuals' seemingly private journeys of faith; they bear witness to the Spirit working in the church's journey, working in the people of God as a whole.

Believers, then, are sources of wisdom for the church. They have something to say, and the church has a responsibility to listen. For when listening to the voice of the faithful, it is often listening to the voice of the Spirit.

So we begin, then, by asking ourselves what we have learned from our years of discipleship. What rays of light have touched our benighted souls? How has our immersion in sacramental ritual stirred our senses, invoking a surprising trust in the saving mysteries of our faith? Reflecting on these ordinary encounters with ritual and sacrament, with parish community and believers from other faith traditions, indeed with our own memories of blessing and grace, we sense a font of truth, perhaps even of wisdom. And here, honoring our personal past as well as the faith stories of our ancestors, we understand that we have *something to say*. Limited, finite, shortsighted—of course. But such is the case of all human insight and wisdom, even when inspired. What we have to say will regularly need the corrective of the community's wisdom; nevertheless, we have *something to say*.

Most believers, of course, are not prelates, theologians, or scholars of sacred Scripture or church history; they are simply baptized disciples. Speaking to the church—especially church authorities—can be daunting even when speaking from one's personal experience of faithful discipleship. Will our experience of everyday Christian living be taken seriously? Will brother and sister believers respect and even reverence what the windstorms of life have taught us? Many disciples wouldn't dare to speak publicly to the church—even when their voice is at least theoretically acknowledged and welcomed in canonically sanctioned structures such as parish or diocesan councils or at parish or diocesan meetings called precisely to hear the voice of the baptized. There is, as we shall see, simply too much to risk. Nevertheless, there comes a time in the lives of many Christians, I believe, when they feel prompted, even compelled, by the Spirit to speak to the church of their concerns, fears, hopes, and anxieties. If they fail to speak, the church is poorer for it. And they themselves are poorer for it—for such betrayals, minor though they seem at the time, chip away at the soul's integrity.

It is one thing to speak in approval, affirmation, or in defense of church policies, procedures, systems, or structures. Relatively little is risked, and, more often than not, church leaders who have established policies and structures of governance did so at a time when they were judged appropriate for the well ordering of the ecclesial body. However, when policies, systems, or structures have outlived their appropriateness or usefulness and members of the church rise to call for their review or change, it is quite a different matter. Then those who dare to speak risk the criticism of both church leaders and their fellow disciples. This is especially true when the issue in question is neuralgic, when it is a lightening rod for the paralyzing polarization that marks our post-conciliar church. Inevitably charges of disloyalty or dissent—not to mention unorthodoxy—arise. In the present prickly climate, it matters little that our religious history reveals that the church is anything but monolithic in either its teaching or structures. We consider below but two examples of the ever-changing face of the church.

The Church as an Unequal Society

Just over a century ago, a very short time from the church's point of view, Pope St. Pius X insisted that the church is an unequal society made up of pastors and flock. In his words: "So distinct are these categories [of pastor and flock] that with the pastoral body only rests the necessary right and authority for promoting the end of the society [the church] and directing all its members toward that end." Pius continues, "[T]he only duty of the multitude is to allow themselves to be led, and, like a docile flock, to follow the pastors" (Vehementer Nos).

In light of our post-conciliar understanding of the church, Pius X's declaration strikes us as antiquated, proudly paternalistic, and even demeaning. Yet, at least from the fourth century, the fundamental inequality of society went unquestioned. It was a "given," part of the nature of things. There were nobles and commoners, the ruling elite and those who were governed, the landed gentry and indentured servants, the educated and the unlettered, and yes—bishops and their flocks. Philosophers and theologians even proposed that monarchy, with its sharp distinction between king and subjects, was the ideal form of government—indeed the form of government that reflected the will of God. This controlling hegemony continued unchallenged at least until the Enlightenment although the church's monastic tradition instinctively and prophetically envisioned communities of brothers and sisters sharing the common life as equals under the leadership and governance of elected abbots and abbesses.

With the American and French revolutions, western society began to take seriously the fundamental, human dignity and, by implication, equality preached by Jesus of Nazareth and underscored in the New Testament. Paradoxically, the institutional church looked with great suspicion and fear on the democratic and republican initiatives that were radically reshaping Europe and North America. In light of the church's long tradition of an exaggerated distinction between clergy and laity and in light of the violent excesses that followed upon revolution in general and the French Revolution in particular, its fear and suspicion were understandable. Seen in this light, Pius X's vision of the church reflected the unquestioned—and what was thought to be the divinely inspired—ways of centuries past.

In startling contrast with this understanding of the church as a society of unequals, the fathers of the Second Vatican Council taught that the baptized faithful are the church, the people of God. While possessing different roles, responsibilities, charisms, and offices in the church, they are fundamentally full and equal members of the church by and through the grace of baptism and the other sacraments of initiation. This retrieved vision of the church was articulated succinctly by the U.S. bishops' committee on priestly life and ministry's 1982 document, *Fulfilled in Your Hearing*. Echoing the ecclesiology of the council, they wrote that the church is "first and foremost a gathering of those whom the Lord has called into a covenant of peace. . . . In this gathering, as in every other, offices and ministries are necessary, but secondary. The primary reality is Christ in the assembly, the People of God."

The theological gap between these two differing understandings of the church sheds light on a major source of the energy-draining tensions and considerable meanness that characterize the current cultural wars in the church. It also sheds light on why it takes courage to speak in today's post-conciliar world. Many in the church, especially among its institutional leaders, still hold to Pius X's understanding of church and the role of the laity. When this view of the church's essential character is the dominant, controlling one, dialogue is not only judged unnecessary, it is feared. From this perspective, transparency is perceived as an irresponsible concession as if greater openness would be a surrender of the bishops' responsibilities. And when this view of church is staunchly defended, accountability to the flock is judged both unnecessary and dangerous. Nor does the flock—the laity—have any right to participate in the governance of the church, even in ways recognized by canon law and the conciliar documents. When George Talbot, an English priest of the Victorian era, was asked about the role of the laity, he responded: "To hunt, to shoot, to entertain. These matters they understand, but to meddle with ecclesiastical matters they have no right at all." A contemporary but like-minded priest might respond to the same question, "To shop, to golf, to entertain. These matters they understand, but they have no right at all to expect accountability and transparency from church authorities."

Most Catholics would fail to recognize the names of theologians Marie-Dominique Chenu and Yves Congar. These men in particular shaped the renewed theology of the laity that remains one of the cornerstones of Vatican II. Most Catholics, however, would recognize the smug clericalism in Father Talbot's response as profoundly at odds with the role of the laity articulated in the council documents. Without question, the role of the laity cannot be reduced to hunting, shooting, and entertaining. Neither can it be reduced to praying, paying, and obeying. Catholics today are among the best-educated and theologically astute sociological groups in the world. They bristle when it is suggested that they should allow themselves to be led like a docile flock of sheep by their pastors.

Until we take to heart the understanding of the church as fundamentally the baptized communion of Jesus' disciples who possess gifts and talents for the mission of the church freely given by the Spirit, the laity will continue to encounter suspicion and mistrust from church authorities. And the church itself, even after promising transparency and accountability as the American bishops did in the wake of the clergy sexual abuse scandal, will continue to practice denial, dissimulation, and deception. These characteristics simply flow, quite naturally, from an understanding of the church as a society made up of unequals. It is difficult to exaggerate the significance of this theological divide in the current

tensions and "cultural wars" that continue to shake the foundations of our church. To speak "one's truth in love" in the midst of
the present climate of suspicion and hostility demands mature
faith and resolute courage.

Remnants of a Feudal Past

A second factor contributing in a significant manner to our
understanding of why courage is required to speak up in the ecclesial assembly is rooted in the church's feudal remnants. That ves-
tiges of feudalism can be found at the core of the church's structure
should not be surprising. Down through the centuries, the institutional church has borrowed or adopted organizational and structural elements from the secular realm—from the Roman Empire
in the fourth century and from various monarchies in later eras as
well as from the social order and culture of European feudalism.
With Vatican II, the church took a definitive step away from its
feudal heritage—at least in theory. In spite of tenacious curial efforts to maintain the old order, the church, especially when understood as a redemptive community of equals, continues to move, if
ever so slowly, away from its feudal past. While imperial and monarchial elements remain controlling forces in the church's current
structure of governance, we are witnessing in the institutional
church the *unraveling of the last feudal system in the West*. This is
especially the case when we examine the structures of church life
involving clergy and their systems of initiation and control.

Feudalism, historians remind us, was an economic, political,
and social system based on land, loyalty, and the need for security
and protection. Its linchpin was unquestioned loyalty. As a layered
social phenomenon, it was hierarchical in nature. At the lowest
rung of the feudal order, serfs, almost exclusively uneducated
peasants, were allowed to live on the land they worked, the land of
the nobility, and to keep a modest portion of the food they pro-
duced while supplying the necessities of life for their superiors. In
return for their labor, serfs enjoyed the protection of their vassal

from marauders and other invaders. Their lot was difficult. No land, no education, no power, no voice!

Vassals, the next rung up on the feudal social order, were granted use of land and authority over their serfs while providing principally military service to their overlord. Above the vassals, the overlords or lords of the manor, ruled territory granted to them by the king and, in return for their loyalty to him, enjoyed the fruits of their benefices. The entire system was grounded on a rock-hard foundation—in promised loyalty, in fact, homage to one's feudal master or superior. In all feudal systems, loyalty and accountability were always upward: vassals never report to serfs, lords of the manor are never accountable to their vassals. And dialogue, especially dialogue involving serfs, was quite literally unthinkable.

Feudal systems, historians point out, work when the economy is based on land and the lower class, the serfs, remain uneducated and dependent on the protection of their vassal. Feudal systems began to break down with the growth of towns, which allowed numerous serfs, often with considerable difficulty, to flee to the towns and become merchants or skilled in the crafts. With the move from a landed economy to a monied economy, medieval feudalism was doomed. Its link, however, with current church structures is obvious. The pope—the sovereign or king in our parallel structure—grants benefices (i.e., dioceses) to his bishops. The bishops in turn promise obedience, homage, and loyalty to their sovereign, the bishop of Rome. While the church's theology now understands the world's bishops as members of a college of bishops in communion with each other and with the bishop of Rome, the full implications of the collegial nature of the episcopacy remain to be developed. The bishops, in turn, grant benefices (i.e., parishes) to their priests, who promise obedience, homage, and loyalty to the chief shepherd of their diocese. At least from the middle of the nineteenth century in the U.S., parishes were run like fiefdoms. And it is not unusual, even in our post-Vatican II church, to find pastors who still perceive their parish as a benefice or a fiefdom. Even more sobering, some pastors continue to look upon parishioners as more or less uneducated sheep.

The Ambiguity of Feudal Loyalty

Officially, bishops and pastors are not ambitious men. They serve their diocese or parish at the pleasure of the pope or the diocesan bishop respectively. Yet ambition is as much a part of the human condition as sexuality—of itself a more or less neutral psychic reality. Underneath the appearance of humble obedience and gratitude for the ecclesiastical appointments they have received, many bishops aspire for more prestigious and powerful dioceses (fiefdoms) as some pastors aspire for more prestigious and influential parishes. Nor can bishops apply for more preferred dioceses to a Vatican episcopal personnel board as priests apply for available pastorates to their diocesan clergy personnel board. The process appears more fraught with ambiguity and ecclesiastical politics for bishops than it is for the lower clergy. The ambitions of some priests for "plum assignments," however, should not be minimized. For the ambitious priest, careful compliance with the party line is a given. Few risks are taken in meeting the pastoral needs of their people. Homilies that might be perceived as progressive or liberal, even when supported by gospel values and the conciliar documents, are eschewed. The prophetic dimension to the ministry of bishop and pastor may disappear completely. For these bishops and pastors it is ministry "by the numbers."

Recently Cardinals Bernard Gantin and Joseph Ratzinger publicly deplored the unabashed careerism they found common in the ranks of the bishops. Both churchmen know their history—that in the first centuries of the church bishops were considered wedded to their dioceses and aspiring to another ecclesiastical benefice was considered akin to infidelity to one's spouse. The present feudal structure of the church fosters such maneuverings which always shrink the integrity of the bishops and pastors who engage in them. Moreover, such unwholesome striving for ecclesiastical advancement harms the church itself. But this is how feudal, clerical systems work.

Politically, economically, and socially we have moved light-years beyond the feudal systems of centuries past. From an ecclesial perspective, however, and specifically from psychological, structural, and cultural perspectives within the framework of the church, the picture is quite different. Obvious remnants of feudalism, beyond those mentioned above, can be detected without much effort. For example, the feudal system's insistence on loyalty and obedience remains deeply imbedded in the Catholic collective unconscious—at least in the collective unconscious of middle-aged and older Catholics.

Moreover, the traditional "offering" made in gratitude to a pope granting a bishopric or an honorary title such as *monsignor* resounds with echoes of feudalism. To the Western ear these monetary expressions of gratitude smack of "buying" honors, titles, and fiefdoms (dioceses). Would these same titles, honors, and clerical appointments, those outside the circle of clerical culture ask, be bestowed upon individuals who were without the means to make the expected offering to the Holy See? Many think not and they are not just the cynical among us. For long periods of time in the church's history, a major source of income for the Vatican treasury was the monetary offerings sent to Rome by recipients of titles, honors, and benefices granted by the pope. It is the way feudal systems worked.

However, the system sets the stage for widespread abuse for it blurs the lines of distinction between what is the personal property of a bishop or pastor and what belongs properly to the diocese or parish. In accord with feudal practice, bishops and pastors have use of the goods of their respective benefices. They may not legally or canonically own these goods or properties, but they may behave as if they do. At least to some extent, the feudal remnants so evident in church structures explain the arrogance that is perceived in some bishops, pastors, and other church authorities. They come to assume, without necessarily bad faith, that "these are my properties and goods to administer as I see fit" with due attention to those circumstances requiring canonical consultation or approval from committees or councils the bishop or pastor himself has appointed.

It is not uncommon, by way of example, for bishops or pastors to receive gifts from parishioners or business persons such as architects, contractors, and auditors couched in these or similar words: "Bishop (or Father)," while handing him an envelope, "this is for you or for your favorite charity." The ambiguity is built into the system and not infrequently it is exploited. Gifts and other expressions of gratitude and goodwill, if made to the church, are tax deductible items. They are not if made to an individual clergyman for personal use. While many if not most bishops and pastors lead truly simple and unpretentious lives, carefully distinguishing to the best of their ability what belongs to the church and what belongs to them personally, some do not. It should come as little surprise, then, that commentators familiar with the inner workings of the church predict that the next wave of scandals to shake the foundations of the church will be fiscal in nature.

The consequences of the church's feudal structure, therefore, remain widespread and significant. Theologian Peter Phan, examining the teaching office of the church in light of the mutuality inherent to the college of bishops, writes in *Governance, Accountability, and the Future of the Catholic Church*:

> In this context use of the terms "loyalty" and "obedience" to describe the relationship between the local bishop and the bishop of Rome . . . should be avoided to prevent misunderstanding. When used to characterize the attitude of bishops to the pope, these terms inevitably suggest to modern ears oaths of submission of vassals to their lords in a feudal system. In the church "loyalty" is owed to no one but Christ, and a bishop is not beholden to the pope for his episcopal office nor is he the pope's vicar.

The church, of course, offers no physical protection behind castle walls from marauding bands of horsemen nor does it provide the sustenance serfs received for their labors. There remains, nonetheless, a kind of spiritual commerce. In place of feudalism's landed economy, the church offers an economy of grace, promising salvation through the "economy" of the sacraments. A subtle "transaction" takes place between parishioners and the clergy understood as keepers of the sacraments. In return for practicing one's faith, that is, for leading a life of moral rectitude and orthodox belief, and in return for obedience to the teaching office of the church and for its financial support, Catholics are granted the assurance of divine grace, of salvation itself. In the eyes of the serf-faithful, then, the vassal-pastor, and the lord-bishop hold awesome spiritual powers essential for achieving eternal life. Addressing these ecclesial authorities, especially for the laity but even for members of the lower clergy, no matter how respectfully, is fraught with moral anxiety. Believers discover that they must reach deep into their souls to find the courage to speak.

While the ecclesial feudal system is unraveling, it is unraveling in fits and starts. Imperial, monarchical, and feudal practices and protocols continue, as we have seen, well into our modern and postmodern world. Older Catholics remember treating bishops as princes of the church. They remember kissing the rings of prelates, often doing so while dropping to one knee. For this generation of believers, the use of feudal, courtly titles for ecclesial authorities—*your Excellency, your Grace, your Eminence*—were simply givens. And many of today's Catholics are pleased, even honored by association, when their diocesan bishop promotes their pastor as well as other loyal priests for the honorific title of *monsignor*. So ingrained is the feudal, courtly system that the bishops' medieval choir robes of royal purple, quite different from liturgical vestments, are still perceived by many Catholics as appropriate.

There is evidence, however, that more and more of the faithful, including bishops, see the negative aspects of a pseudo-nobility that remains a major legacy of the feudal structures still operative in the church. African bishop Nestor Ngoy Katahwa of the Congo told his brother bishops at a 2001 Vatican conference on the episcopacy:

With our title of "princes of the church," we are led to cultivating the search for human honors and privileges, while the king, in reference to whom we are princes, finds his glorification on the cross. . . . We are more at ease with the powerful and the rich than with the poor and the oppressed. And the fact that we maintain sole legislative, executive and judicial powers is a temptation for us to act like dictators, more so inasmuch as our mandate has no limitations.

The Role of Authority

The critique offered here of feudal elements in the church's structure is easily misread, especially in some Vatican circles and chancery offices, as furthering a creeping democratization of the church and therefore as an assault on the authority of the church. Outside the circle of doctrine, the church's history reflects greater and lesser degrees of democratization. Moreover, the church has been healthiest when it has taken seriously the wisdom of the faithful. The true threats to the authority of the church more often than not arise from the myopic vision of church leaders themselves who believe they alone are the guardians of faith and the Christian tradition. Their arrogance, coupled with their mistrust of and disregard for the voice of the faithful—revealed so painfully in their handling of the clergy sexual abuse scandals— has profoundly weakened their credibility and moral authority in the eyes of their fellow Christians and society at large.

Criticism, therefore, of the church's current forms of governance and calls for structural reform must emerge from a profound commitment and respect for the authority of both the gospel and the teaching office of the church. Loyalty, obedience, and respect remain essential for the order of the church and for the implementation of the church's mission. There will always be some form of ordered structure within any church claiming a teaching office and ecclesial authority. But a healthy, vital church insists on authority that is *authoritative* rather than *authoritarian*. It insists on church

leaders whose efforts to lead by the light of the gospel are apparent
and whose lifestyles reflect gospel simplicity. It insists on leaders
and pastors who are at home with the powerless as well as the
powerful and influential, who possess a passion for justice and
peace. It insists on leaders who "do not make their authority felt,"
but rather understand their pastoral responsibilities as service to
the people of God and to the liberating freedom of the gospel.

It would be a mistake, I believe, to assume that modern-day disciples of Jesus no longer need authority. Paul Tillich, one of the most
influential philosophers and theologians of the twentieth century,
noted the danger here: "He who tries to be without authority tries
to be like God who alone is by Himself. And like everyone who tries
to be like God, he is thrown down into self-destruction, be it a single
human being, be it a nation, be it a period of history like our own."
What is clearly needed in today's church is an authority and teaching office that rings true—an authority that is grounded in charism
and grace, an authority rooted in humility and honesty, an authority that preaches the freedom of the gospel. Those holding such
gospel authority would be alert to its dark side: the tendency to exercise it arbitrarily. They would know how to listen.

Seen from the historical analysis outlined above, the feudal
structures still ingrained in the church explain, to a considerable
degree, the church's faltering authority and growing authoritarianism. These same remnants of feudal culture also explain the
confounding lack of candor, honesty, accountability, and transparency so painfully evident since the latest round of clergy abuse
scandals that erupted in January 2002. And these remnants have
contributed greatly to the secrecy, arrogance, denial, and hardball
legal tactics that have come to be associated with a large number
of our bishops and church authorities. Moreover, we find here the
roots of clericalism—those ingrained attitudes of privileged status, of exemption and exclusivity, that make dialogue between the
faithful and church leaders so painfully difficult.

In the absence of honest communication between bishops and
the folks in the pews, the present crisis of leadership was bound to

move inexorably to its present level of mutual mistrust. The bishops with their diminished if not lost credibility wait for their long
Lent to pass, naively expecting things to return to the way they
were before the clergy abuse cases rocked the church. At the same
time, the laity wait, perhaps also naively, for the promised accountability and transparency.

What both church authorities and parishioners seem to miss
or dismiss is the shaping, controlling power of feudalism's culture.
Culture, we now understand, is not simply a complex of social
forces that more or less directly influence our values, our ways of
perceiving and thinking, and our decisions. While we do, in a
sense, *have* a culture it is more accurate to say that culture *has*
us. We are, it has been said, *buried alive in culture.* How else explain
the scandalous and incomprehensible behavior of so many of our
bishops when presented with reliable knowledge that their priests
were betraying the most vulnerable members of the church?
These were and are fundamentally good men, even very good
men. As bishops, they were unquestionably loyal to the institutional church; but they were also, with few notable exceptions,
men who possessed a genuine pastoral concern for their people.
But it was the clerical, feudal culture to which they owed their
identity and position that betrayed them—co-opted them. The
historically conditioned system that worked so well for these episcopal leaders was perceived to be "of God." They were, after all,
men of God committed whole-heartedly to a church "of God." It is
a short step to see the system—the feudal, clerical culture—as "of
God." It must be protected, lest scandal be given, lest the integrity
and reputation of the church and its priesthood be tarnished—*at
all costs.* The irony, of course, is that such culturally imbedded beliefs and attitudes flirt with idolatry.

I am not proposing that the numerous decisions of our bishops that put thousands of our children and teenagers in harm's
way were free of personal culpability. I am proposing that the
church's feudal culture is also a culprit, a major culprit, in the
scandal that continues to shake the very institutional foundations

of the church. This remains a major factor in the ongoing cry heard from laity, clergy—including high ranking prelates—and vowed religious for structural reform.

The Promise of Respect and Obedience

While the laity struggle to claim their rightful place in church dialogue, there is already a model for them. At the beginning of the ordination ritual for the priesthood, a deacon reads aloud the name of each candidate for Holy Orders. As his name is read, the seminarian responds: "Present" (I am here, I am ready to accept this call to priestly service). When I was ordained in 1965, the ordination ritual was in Latin. My classmates and I responded after our name was called, *"Adsum"* (I am present). After the imposition of hands by the bishop and the attending clergy, each newly ordained priest kneels before his bishop, places his hands in the hands of the bishop, and promises him and his successors respect and obedience. It is a powerful, moving ritual of faith, loyalty, and homage. And its feudal origin is unmistakable.

Following this promise of respect and obedience to his "lord bishop," for a priest to speak candidly and freely to his bishop— this successor of the apostles who has such life-shaping power over his priests—demands considerable moral courage. The same psychological and spiritual control and power, perhaps to a lesser degree, keeps the laity from speaking easily and without fear to their bishop. Of course, it always requires courage to speak to power. But in the church it should be somewhat easier to speak from one's faith-filled experience to church authorities called to be servants of the servants of God. Speaking to church authorities, nevertheless, requires courage, and sometimes heroic courage. It need not be this way.

Perhaps it is time for the laity to steal a line from the ordination ritual. I believe it is time for the laity to stand boldly but humbly in the assembly of the church and declare in a firm and clear voice, *"Adsum." We are present. With our ordained brothers we stand ready to offer our talents and gifts to further the life of the church and the mission of the church.* And because feudal structures tend to keep those on the lower rungs of the system less than fully adult, in some ways perpetual adolescents, it is necessary to continue: *And we fully expect to be treated as adult members of the church. We fully expect to know the true extent of the abuse scandal. We fully expect to know its true financial cost, and we fully expect to have a more explicit role and voice, commensurate with our experience, gifts, and competence, in the governance of the church. Let this declaration of ecclesial adulthood, this* Adsum *we speak from our hearts, be a promise of obedience, loyalty, and fidelity to the gospel, to our conscience, and to our church.*

The time also has come for priests to stand with their parishioners and declare a second *Adsum*. It is time for them to look deep into their hearts for the courage to boldly yet humbly say, *We promise obedience, loyalty, and fidelity to the gospel, to our conscience, and to the church.* Only then will the people of God find the courage to speak.

Clericalism's Link to Feudalism

Inexorably linked with the church's feudal culture, we have seen, is a clerical culture deeply imbedded in the individual and collective unconscious of the clergy, and, by extension, in the unconscious of the laity who unwittingly support the cultures in which they live, as it were, "buried alive." In *Sacred Silence: Denial and the Crisis in the Church,* I treated at some length the important role clericalism—the almost inevitable outgrowth of clerical culture—plays in the turmoil marking the church at the turn of the century. Clericalism, as commonly understood today, is fundamentally an attitude found in clergy who have made their status as priests and bishops more important than their status as baptized disciples of Jesus the Christ. In doing so, there emerges in their individual and collective psyche a sense of privilege, preferment, and entitlement, which in turn breeds aloofness and an ecclesiastical elitism. Clergy captured by this kind of purple-hewed seduction are incapable of seeing that it freezes their humanity. As Orthodox theologian Alexander Schmemann observes: "Clericalism suffocates; it makes part of itself into the whole sacred character of the church; it makes its power a sacred power to control, to lead, to administer; a power to perform sacraments, and, in general, it makes any power a 'power given to me!'" (The Journals of Father Alexander Schmemann).

So intimately are these two cultures connected that it is reasonable to describe their melding as two sides of the same coin. Because each culture complements and reinforces the other, their combined influence, which on one level remains invisible, is, nonetheless, staggering. One sad, even tragic, effect of this subtle but pervasive influence is the curtailing of honest dialogue and conversation between laity and church authorities. In the feudal, clerical world, even clearly non-dogmatic disciplines, policies, practices, and traditions, such as mandatory celibacy for diocesan priests and the process for naming bishops, are treated with such external reverence that they take on the mantel of doctrine. To question them is to be judged disloyal. To call for open discussion and dialogue about these issues is to be dismissed as a radical, dissenting liberal harboring an agenda designed to undermine the church.

Only brave hearts break through these invisible but reinforced cultural barriers "to speak the truth in love," as St. Catherine of Siena challenged popes, princes, and the people of God to do centuries ago. And when brave hearts do speak, as the recent clerical scandals have demonstrated, they are more often than not dismissed by church authorities as disloyal dissenters. To the contrary, they are believers accepting the responsibilities of adult members in the church.

When the prioress of the Akron Dominican sisters, Elizabeth Ann Schaefer, died days before Christmas in 2003, I stood in the midst of her grieving sisters, family, and friends at the gravesite service. The ritual included the following prayer: "We praise you, O God of truth and life, who called Libby (as she was known) and each one of us to our mission of preaching the Word. Set your power free in us who remain, so that nourished by contemplation and supported by community, our family and friends, we may faithfully continue to hear, to remember, and to proclaim the Word that gives life. Like Dominic, our brother, and Catherine, our sister in Christ, and like Libby, our sister in time, may we be *fearless* in speaking the truth, undaunted in the pursuit of reform, and generous in caring for the poor and afflicted" (italics added).

As we have seen, only the fearless of heart, with their courage nourished by contemplation and the support of community and friends, dare to "speak the truth in love."

CHAPTER TWO

THE HUMILITY TO LISTEN

In humility is perfect freedom.

—Thomas Merton

People hearing without listening . . . .

—Simon and Garfunkel

Come near, O Nations, and hear;
be attentive, O peoples!
Let the earth and what fills it listen, . . .

—Isaiah 34: 1

FROM THE EARLIEST ACCOUNTS OF THE CHURCH, seen especially in the First Letter to Timothy, one of the primary responsibilities of bishops is to teach. But it is both interesting and disturbing to discover that bishops, as *the* teachers of the faith, are to forego situations that would give the impression that they are in any formal sense students. Their identity as *teachers*, apparently, precludes even the appearance of assuming the role of *student*. When bishops meet for instruction and various forms of continuing education, they do so under the rubric of a "consultation" or "retreat." Perhaps this is little more than an episcopal conceit supported by the ecclesiology of Pope Pius X who taught, as we saw in the previous chapter, that the laity were to follow their ordained shepherds (and teachers) as docile sheep. Rather than a relatively harmless clerical conceit, this episcopal protocol and the theology supporting it remain significant obstacles to honest and authentic dialogue between the laity and the hierarchy as well as between the lower clergy and the hierarchy. For we now understand that in a society of unequals, teaching and governing models inevitably become paternalistic.

By training and instinct, teachers listen carefully to the questions of their students in order to respond with appropriate answers. And pastors listen for the core or essence of a problem brought to them by parishioners so that they might offer sound counsel and advice that will help to solve the problem in question. Listening both for the questions and problems of the laity is, unquestionably, a necessary and important skill for pastoral ministers, priests, and bishops. The baptized have every right to expect from their teachers and pastors clear answers to their questions and wise counsel in addressing their personal and family issues.

While bishops represent a small percentage of the church's pastoral ministers—there are approximately 380 bishops leading and serving sixty-seven million U.S. Catholics—their voice and ministry touch the lives of most practicing believers. Bishops believe sincerely, I am convinced, that they do listen to the voice of their faithful—however they listen more often than not for the question raised or the problem presented in order to respond as teacher and pastor. But do they also listen to be *informed* and possibly *transformed*? Listening to be informed and possibly transformed requires a certain openness of soul, a trust that God's Spirit is freely given, is, if you will, loose in the world. "To each person the manifestation of the Spirit is given for the common good" (1 Cor 12:7).

Especially since the first Vatican Council, which crystallized the church's profound fear of the emerging historical consciousness, bishops have learned to listen defensively. This pre-Vatican II episcopal ethos, still the controlling ethos for large numbers of bishops, judges the principles of freedom, progress, and democracy as inherently dangerous to the faith. For these church leaders, John Henry Newman's *Essay on the Development of Christian Doctrine* remains problematic. In their minds, Christian belief is fundamentally static and ahistorical. Wherever this theology of the church becomes the controlling ecclesiology, the ability to listen is compromised—even blocked. If one is convinced that he or she possesses the absolute, complete, and unchanging revealed truth of God, what really is there to learn? What really motivates one to listen? Only to persuade, to answer questions, to offer advice.

What disturbed and concerned many Vatican and American prelates about the U.S. bishops' initiative in the early 1980s to write a pastoral letter on the role of women in the church were the extensive listening sessions that preceded the numerous drafts of their letter. The bishops charged with drafting the pastoral letter had determined to listen carefully to the concerns of U.S. Catholic women. Structuring listening sessions for the writers of the pastoral, of course, was logical, prudent, necessary, and respectful of the important role women play in the church. But when individuals in leadership believe they have nothing to learn from the lives and experiences of those "under" them, listening to the laity as adult dialogue partners is determined to be unnecessary—and worse—an opportunity for airing progressive notions and ideas. Following the decision to write a pastoral letter on the role of women, a few American bishops initiated listening sessions in their respective dioceses. These men elicited the "concern" of Vatican authorities, no matter that such listening sessions reflected the ecclesiology of the Second Vatican Council.

While bishops play a central and essential role in the teaching office of the church, they are, like the rest of the faithful, disciples of Jesus the Christ. As disciples, they too sit at the feet of the Master. And, as disciples, they too are meant to encounter the wisdom of God in their fellow disciples, even those disciples not called to the ministry of bishop. If we believe the church is always in need of reform and renewal, are not all members of the church, including those charged with leadership, students in need of learning—students attentive to and respectful of the teaching office of the church, but also open to the work of scholars, to the *sensus fidelium*, to the development of doctrine?

When Priests Listen

When it comes to listening, priests confront the same forces that challenge bishops—perhaps only to a lesser degree. With their average age in the early to mid-sixties, most priests have been trained in pre-Vatican II seminaries where they were instructed to embrace a static, ahistorical understanding of the nature of the church. When individuals are convinced they possess the fullness of revealed truth, it affects the way they listen. So, like their bishops, they too have been trained to listen for questions to be answered and for problems to be solved. This kind of listening, we have already noted, is at the heart of their ministry as priests. Our most successful pastors, I am convinced, have learned to listen not only for the questions and problems of their parishioners but also for the voice of God, the "rumors of angels," that regularly can be discerned in the thicket of the joys and sorrows, the successes and sufferings, the fidelities and betrayals of the faithful to whom they minister.

Priests hold front row seats to the multiple dramas of grace unfolding in the lives of the children, women, and men that make up their parish. They are entrusted with secrets and stories told to no one else. They witness, often daily, in the lives of ordinary people a wide spectrum of human suffering: crippling depressions, crushing anxieties, confusing doubts, broken hearts, as well as heroic courage, enduring faith, and unflagging hope. Few priests, perhaps only those steeped in clericalism, fail to be moved—and informed and transformed—by these encounters with grace. Sometimes they know they have been instruments of healing and grace, "earthen vessels" of God's love, and the realization humbles, always humbles them. For these priests, listening has become a matter of the heart, even a sacred art.

Yet there is no denying that priests must own their own failures to listen. Some, along with a number of bishops, have failed to listen nondefensively to the reports of sexual abuse at the hands of their brother priests, to the anguish of parents and siblings of the violated and betrayed. Others may listen well to their parishioners but fail to listen to the veiled calls for help from family, friends, and brother priests. What may be the most difficult form of listening for many priests is related to the tending of their own souls. It is a form of self-pastoral care easily overlooked as their work hours expand and their ranks thin. Listening, as care of one's soul, requires the ability to sit still long enough to hear what is rising up from one's own depths.

By way of example, from my work with priests I have come to see that many of them are grieving without being explicitly aware that the restlessness and emptiness they feel is grief. With the rest of the human family, priests grieve the passages of life—the loss of their youth, their middle years, the health they once enjoyed as younger men. Some grieve the subtle loss of their integrity, the small treasons occasioned by fear or cowardice. Others grieve the wife and family sacrificed to mandatory celibacy. Most today grieve the loss of trust and confidence which followed the sexual betrayal of countless children and young people. With the lay faithful, they lament the failed leadership of American bishops whose inability to listen to the anguished voices of women has impoverished the church.

Priests today speak of the discouragement and loss of morale that occur when their bishops fail to listen to them. While numerous bishops have complained about the growing centralization of authority in the church in recent years and their own frustrations at not being heard by Vatican congregations, their priests question whether these same bishops are really listening to them. Overworked and misunderstood, their concerns about the dramatic drop in the number of priests and seminarians is met with a rejoinder from their bishop to pray for vocations to the priesthood and to recruit more actively. Their requests for discussion and review of mandatory celibacy for diocesan priests of the Latin rite are blithely deflected with paternalistic cliches.

Especially since the latest eruption of clergy sexual abuse that marked the first days of 2002, priests are now listening with a new openness to each other and to their parishioners. As they listen, a considerable number have discovered a long-dormant strength and courage to "speak their truth in love" to their ecclesial superiors. These brave priests take hope in the words of Hans Küng: "One parish priest does not count in the diocese, five are given attention, 50 are invincible" (quoted in David Gibson's *The Coming Catholic Church*). At the troubled beginning of the new millennium, priests acknowledge their need to listen carefully to the wisdom of the gospel, to the lessons of their pastoral experience, to the experience of their parishioners, and indeed to the voice of their bishops.

When the Lay Faithful Listen

Still considered by some church authorities as more or less serfs, by others as the simple faithful, and still others as less likely than the hierarchy to be inspired by the Spirit, the laity have little to lose in listening from their hearts. They listen with a poverty of spirit that purifies and readies them to face the sad realities of their wounded church.

The humility necessary for listening with one's heart and soul may well be a more common virtue among the nonordained than the ordained. To be sure, there are poor listeners seated in the pews as well as poor listeners among those who occupy the presider's chair or the bishop's chair. There are fewer cultural and structural obstacles, however, to effective listening among the laity. Especially among blue-collar Catholics there exists a keen ability to balance their legendary fidelity to the church that eased the burdens of their immigrant ancestors with a discerning eye for what is real, down to earth, and unpretentious. Their understanding of the faith may be more rudimentary than that of fellow parishioners with college degrees, but their ability to listen for the saving and sustaining word of God is second to none.

Not only do American Catholics listen with their hearts and souls, they listen with their minds—many with well-educated minds. On any given Sunday, a priest may find seated in the assembly women and men with graduate degrees in theology or sacred Scripture. In some parishes professors of theology, religion, homiletics, and the Bible can be found in the congregation. These are but a few of the indicators pointing to a reality that some church authorities have yet to fully comprehend: the Catholic laity of the twenty-first century have socially and economically "arrived" and are among the world's best-educated people. Many parishioners have studied theology at the college level, while a growing number hold master of theology or master of divinity degrees. Others read respected journals such as *America, Commonweal,* and *The Tablet* as well as books addressing the current crises in the church. They have learned to think, reason, evaluate, and discern—and to reflect on their experiences as disciples. Their reflection has taught them to listen for the voice of God in the rhythms of their personal and communal journeys of faith. They thirst for good preaching and meaningful programs of adult education. They receive with suspicion, if not incredulity, authoritarian pronouncements and doctrinal and disciplinary teachings not supported by sound scriptural and theological sources or that fail to take into consideration their life experiences as faithful Catholics. They wince at clichéd responses to their concerns and questions. With overwhelming sadness, they see spouses, children, and friends turn away from the church—some explicitly and formally, others leaving "in place"—members of the church in name only. Those who remain stay in spite of their discouragement and anger, anger galvanized by the bishops' handling of the clergy abuse scandals—their staying a tribute to the power of the church's sacramental life and to the fidelity of their ancestors, teachers, and catechists.

In spite of their anger and disillusionment, the Catholic faithful, for the most part, continue to remain in the church and listen patiently for a word from the Lord. They listen for words of understanding and inclusion from church leaders. They listen for invitations from their bishops that will allow them to speak candidly of their concerns. They wait for indications of the accountability and transparency promised by the bishops at their 2002 Dallas meeting dealing with the abuse crisis. And with undying hope, they listen for yet another announcement of "a year of favor from the Lord" (Luke 4:19).

The Elusive Virtue

Years ago I heard a story that illustrates the elusive nature of humility. There was an elderly man known to all in the village for his remarkable humility. So moved were the elders of the village by the humble ways of this simple and good man that they decided to bestow upon him a medal for his extraordinary humility. One day, not too long after receiving his medal, the old man decided to wear it. And the elders of the village took it back! We all seem to know people who are proud of their humility. It's one of those virtues we dare not claim, even privately, lest we betray ourselves in the very claiming of it. Even the essence of the virtue is somewhat mysterious. Media evangelists insist that humility does not mean thinking less of yourself but rather thinking of yourself less.

It seems that humility, like many other virtues, is best pursued indirectly. Rather than overtly striving to be a humble person, Thomas Merton encouraged his readers to seek the grace to be their true selves as distinct from their false selves. The false self, he wrote, is our ego-self, the self that our culture insists must be asserted and protected at all costs. It's the self that is quick to be offended, the self that is incessantly comparing and competing, striving to get ahead of the pack, and ever restless and unsatisfied. Our true self, on the other hand, is the self that is hidden in God, the self that is the spark of the divine. This self "in communion" accepts who he or she is— friend of God and beloved member of the people of God. As the true self emerges in an individual, comparisons are infrequent and competition, when engaged in, is for the shear joy of doing one's best. Humble people live more of their lives than not in their true selves. When their false selves emerge, as is the case with our human condition, their influence is short-lived. Humility is important here, for as soon as individuals sense they are grounded in the true self, the false self is poised to surface.

Merton, more than any other modern spiritual writer, has identified the inherent link that exists between humility and freedom. "In humility," he writes, "is perfect freedom." Humble people are freed from undue care about how they are doing in the eyes of others. They are freed from the fear of failure, of making fools of themselves. There is a spontaneity evident in their lives, a graceful freedom to live fully in the present. Humble people know, without undue anxiety, when to take prudent risks. In a culture that celebrates radical individualism, they possess a keen sense that they belong, that they are members of numerous, life-giving communities—family, church, neighborhood, civic community, society itself. Their very sense of belonging frees them from undue introspection and self-doubt. In a word, they are free to be the men or women God has called them to be. And because they are not weighted down by the shackles of egocentricity, that is by the false self, they listen with an openness of mind and heart. Furthermore, the true self senses the connection between humility and truthfulness—that somehow the humble of heart both listen and speak with a greater purity of spirit that remains open to the wisdom and truth of others—what theologian Margaret Farley calls the "grace of self doubt."

Humility liberates in numerous ways. It is the virtue that leads from hearing to listening—that allows us to discover the embers of truth in theologies and ecclesial positions different from our own. It is suspicious of all ideologies and instinctively searches for the true and the good. For these reasons alone it is disturbing to hear Catholics describe their bishop as arrogant. To the extent their perception is accurate, the bishop's ability to listen is gravely limited.

Arrogance and the Ability to Listen

Since the conversion of Constantine in the early fourth century, the church's organizational structure, governance, and even forms of address and dress have been either copied from or influenced by the imperial, monarchical, and feudal cultures in which the church existed and flourished. Moreover, at various times in its history, the church perceived itself as a holy empire or a divine monarchy. Imperial and monarchial systems, as with all strictly hierarchical cultures, cannot help but sow seeds of arrogance among those in superior positions. Dressed in the fashions of society's ruling elite, addressed with titles attributed to nobility and even royalty, high ranking church authorities assumed in many cases the manner, airs, and poses of their secular counterparts. Only the authentically humble among them were capable of escaping the temptation to claim personal superiority. The church's history, of course, records countless examples of humble, saintly men and women in the highest strata of both secular and ecclesiastical empires, monarchies, and fiefdoms. Recent popes such as John XXIII and John Paul I recall humble pontiffs and prelates of ages past. Still, cultures with explicit class distinctions present serious challenges to those in positions of authority desiring to eschew arrogance in all its forms.

Our concern here is not the prevalence of arrogance among some bishops and church authorities—although wherever arrogance is found among church ministers and leaders, the mission of the church and witness to the gospel suffer. Rather the attention we accord to arrogant attitudes in church leaders is meant to emphasize the impact of such haughtiness on their ability to listen. The same concern holds for the laity and lower clergy. Arrogant attitudes and behaviors, wherever and whenever they are encountered, inhibit the ability to listen.

Long before the reign of Pope Pius X, which bridged the nineteenth and twentieth centuries, the church understood itself and was perceived by outsiders as a society of unequals made up of pastors and sheep—an understanding that held until Vatican II. The influence of the pre-Vatican II ecclesiology, though officially transcended by the council's teaching, remains to this day. The unequal society mentality was evident in the manner church authorities tragically mishandled the clergy abuse scandal. Wherever the church continues to be understood as a society of unequals, there will be little concern for accountability and transparency and for the healthy expression of opinion and thought. To the extent the "flock and shepherd" theology influences the church's style of governance, the open-minded listening essential for real dialogue will be hindered.

Even when the revised Code of Canon Law underscores the right and at times the duty of the faithful "to manifest to their sacred pastors their opinion on matters which pertain to the good of the Church and to make their opinion known to the rest of the Christian faithful" (c. 212, 3), it interjects a note of inequality. Here and elsewhere in church documents bishops and other ordained ministers are referred to as *sacred* pastors. Are the lay faithful, by implication, non-sacred? Through the waters of baptism all the baptized are consecrated, made sacred, by their immersion in the life of Jesus Christ in the power of the Holy Spirit. When Canon Law emphasizes the sacred character and role of prelates and priests, listening and speaking, the fundamental elements of dialogue, become skewed. While roles in the church are clearly distinct and vary in their ministerial responsibilities, the council teaches clearly the fundamental dignity and equality of all the baptized: "[I]f by the will of Christ some are made teachers, dispensers of the mysteries, and shepherds on behalf of others, yet all share a true equality with regard to the dignity and to the activity common to all the faithful for the building up of the Body of Christ" (*Lumen Gentium*, 32). Whenever this fundamental equality is overshadowed by lingering remnants of monarchical and feudal cultures of inequality, toxic tensions surface in the ecclesial community that lead to various forms of clericalism, legalism, triumphalism, and authoritarianism. In this milieu, understandably, it is difficult beyond words for the lay faithful to speak their minds with any hope of an honest hearing.

Ideology

Humility, Merton and other writers propose, is the great liberator of the soul. And so it is. It also is the great liberator of the intellect—for it frees us from the tyranny of ideology. The humble woman or man senses, *knows* with the knowledge of the heart, that our various attempts to systematize God's revelation into theologies and schools of theology with their refined doctrinal formulations have their place in organized religion. The humble believer, however, has discovered through fits and starts, through the estrangements and reconciliations of discipleship, that the heart of religion is relational—our mysterious union with God and creation in God's freely communicated self that Christians call grace. Freed from the rationalism of imperial, monarchical, and hierarchical ideologies, the humble individual, with or without theological training, knows what really matters and treasures that which matters most.

Humble people see through the rationalism, dogmatism, and legalism of the ideologue, whether religious, political, or intellectual. They have learned to look for goodness and truth in every human encounter. They listen well and respectfully to those from different "parties," whether religious or political. The tone of their measured speech draws listeners to consider the particular insight or point of view which they raise. When those who listen disagree, speakers with humble and contemplative spirits listen respectfully and non-defensively. Possessing the "grace of self doubt," they are seldom threatened or made anxious by ecumenical and inter-faith dialogue and cooperation. Most fundamentally of all, humble people know God is bigger than their religion, bigger than any political platform, bigger than the scandalous intramural church battles that have bred so much violence and hatred.

It is important to distinguish between the authentic faith of humble disciples and the shrill orthodoxy of religious ideologues. Humble disciples, from a state of inner peace and regard for others, invite conversation and dialogue while religious ideologues are determined to convince others whom they perceive as opponents if not enemies. The former listen to be informed and possibly transformed. The latter listen to identify error and correct it. The former "speak the truth in love"; the latter declare the truth with might.

Conclusion

Perhaps the current sexual, episcopal, and financial scandals plunging the U.S. church into its present unprecedented crisis may be the impetus necessary to deflate the arrogant and self-righteous and to rediscover "the ennoblement of the humble" *(Lord of the Rings)*. The faithful, though apparently far from rebellion, remain discouraged and frustrated, searching for signs of real leadership and listening for words of integrity from their own lay leaders as well as their appointed pastors and bishops. As if in exile, they wait and listen for prophets of deliverance.

Learning to listen, especially in the midst of the current crisis, demands more than psychic energy and focused concentration, as important as these factors are to honest conversation and dialogue. What is required is a contemplative heart, a humility that awakens the soul to the essence of Christian faith that lies beneath and beyond the various cultures and ideologies that breed contention and division. Listening from the heart, like so many other aspects of living in community and society, is the result of conversion, the working of grace that dissolves the arrogance of triumphalism and the superiority of clericalism. Here, as in every period of crisis, the faithful, both clergy and lay, must face the inevitable tensions of church life seeking the wisdom to listen humbly and to speak bravely.

CHAPTER THREE

LOVE THAT DARES
TO QUESTION

What has gone wrong? In what ways is the Church defective? How are
we failing in our call to be and to bring good news?

—Bishop John Heaps

Be patient toward all that is unsolved in your heart and try to love the
questions themselves.

—Rainer Maria Rilke

SIMPLY TO BE HUMAN, we know, is to wonder, to question. In doing
so we honor the divine programming of our minds that, as the de-
fault setting, asks *why*? We also have come to know that often the
most fundamental, unsettling, and critical questions are asked by
children who have not yet learned to fear asking questions. But
soon children learn what adults have come to know: be wary of
questions. It's often safer to stifle the urge to ask the fundamental
questions that easily disturb the fragile surface calm of our everyday lives. Children learn early enough that questions that deal
with important matters—like religion—easily provoke anxiety
and fear and even violence. Fundamental questions: *Where did we
come from? Why are we here? What is the meaning of life? What
is God like?* are religious questions that raise in turn the foundational question about the nature of revelation and how we come to
know revelation and define it. These existential and theological
questions take us to the edge of our defenses behind which we
struggle to control and husband the sea of anxiety that is the lot of

the human condition. Fundamental questions take us to that place where we would rather not be. They take us to the desert of doubt and to windstorms of anxiety. Spiritual doubt and spiritual anxiety disturb our conscious tranquility as nothing else.

So it is that we have learned early on in life to repress our doubts and questions—not necessarily about the existence of God or the saving role of Jesus the Christ—but our doubts and questions relating to the mystery of God and our relationship to God as mediated by the church. For the most part, we leave them to the philosophers, poets, preachers, and theologians. We take refuge in the epic stories of faith and fidelity passed on to us from our long dead ancestors that bring some semblance of order out of our spiritual confusion. Being religious is one way, perhaps *the* way, most of us come to terms with the existential and theological questions of life.

Having gained some degree of tranquility and order, it is understandable that we are wary of questions that threaten our philosophical and religious security. In Catholic circles, questions dealing with religious belief, human sexuality, church governance, and the role of women in leadership, for example, are fraught with danger. Unless we are certain of the company we are in, it is thought best not to go there.

It is not surprising then that Australian bishop John Heaps titled his 1997 book *A Love That Dares to Question*. Questioning in today's church, so marked by the cultural wars brought to high pitch in the years following the Second Vatican Council, is risky. Some in high church circles believe that if you love the church you don't question it, you accept it. For these leaders loyalty to the church means the same thing: one does not question it. After all, the reasoning goes, the bishops are the successors of the apostles. Loyalty to the church, therefore, means trusting the church's leaders. In this climate one who questions *dares* to question.

Moreover, as we have seen in chapter 1, the feudal remnants of the church cast a negative light on questions—and the questioners —that come from "below." Unless the questions are questions seeking information, clarification, or counsel, they may be judged

disrespectful or even impudent. In feudal systems one always dares
to question. The same can be said for rigid hierarchical systems,
whether of a secular nature or of an ecclesiastical nature. What
makes loving, loyal questioning in today's church all the more daring is a "creeping infallablism" that reduces a broad range of issues
unrelated to revealed truths such as historically conditioned structures, policies, disciplines, and traditions as linked to divine doctrine.
Such non-doctrinal church issues become, in effect, matters of doctrine. To question them is not only disloyal from this perspective, it
brings the questioner under suspicion of being unfaithful.

Undoubtedly, it is much safer to raise questions in today's
church than in centuries past when dissent and even the questioning of church teaching could lead to imprisonment, torture, and
sometimes death. The church, historians remind us, went so far as
to institutionalize a very different kind of questioning in the thir-
teenth century with the establishment of the Inquisition which
continued in existence until the late nineteenth century. But the
questioning here institutionalized was of a clearly different sort.
The officers of the Inquisition were empowered to question—with
the prodding of papally sanctioned torture—suspected dissenters.
They questioned, of course, not for greater understanding or knowledge or wisdom (they believed they already possessed the truth of
the deposit of faith), but for evidence of unholy questioning of
doctrinal beliefs. As noted above, in feudal, hierarchical systems,
serious questioning itself is considered dangerous. By definition
these cultures are beyond the "grace (and humility) of self-doubt."
The only questioning tolerated came from those in authority, and
its purpose was to ferret out those who questioned or challenged
the reigning orthodoxy.

Questioning in these circumstances was indeed daring.
Copernicus and the scientists he influenced placed themselves in
danger by questioning the reigning cosmology that was understood by church authorities to be grounded in divine revelation.
To challenge, as many saints and mystics did, the avarice and cor-
ruption of the papacy of their day was clearly courageous, even

heroic. Those who dared to question and confront the obvious abuses of clerics and prelates often suffered terrible fates. The Inquisition has been suppressed, but the suppression of even honest and faithful questioning of non-dogmatic elements and practices in the church continues.

Daring to Question

The history of the church is to a considerable degree a history of daring questions, either explicit or implicit. Paul's confrontation with Peter and the Jerusalem church regarding the necessity of Gentile converts submitting to Jewish cultural and religious traditions and laws raised a fundamental question for the early followers of Jesus. From Catherine of Siena questioning the self-serving machinations of a pope to modern-day believers questioning the restricted roles for women in ministry, the vitality of the church has been sustained by challenges and questions put to those in leadership. Healthy individuals question how they might live more authentic, faithful, and integrated lives. Healthy institutions understand the necessity of raising questions about how things are being done and of proposing possibly better ways to get them done. The "grace of self-doubt" applies to institutions, even divinely inspired institutions.

Bishop Heaps understood that to question even out of love and loyalty requires courage. For questions, as we have seen, break through the mirage of surface calm revealing issues that threaten current structures of power and the order necessary for the mission of the church. To raise them is to risk criticism and even assault. For some, it means risking one's job, one's career, even one's place at the eucharistic table. At the same time, raising questions in the church today requires humility. One may be misguided, misinformed, or just plain wrong. One's self-respect and personal dignity are often on the line when a question is asked, when an issue is raised. But the humble person takes the risk believing that nothing can separate us from the love of God in Christ Jesus.

Humble people don't always have to be right. But they do want to be faithful—and people of integrity. In this light, not to question unmasks cowardice and pride.

Lingering Questions, Daunting Issues

In *Sacred Silence: Denial and the Crisis in the Church,* I tried to explore the source of the denial and unholy silence practiced by church authorities in the face of issues and crises that were seen by the faithful as undeniable. What was it, I asked, that prompted the denial and dissimulation with which church officials responded to the concerns and questions of large numbers of Catholics. Here I want to probe possible explanations for the church's reluctance to address more forthrightly the questions and issues of contemporary believers. The issues raised below are framed as questions, either explicit or implicit, which in turn have elicited in some cases answers and in other cases silence or denial from church officials. Often the answers given as well as the denials asserted are telling.

Why Celibacy Is Defended

Because of its sacramental character, the reputation and status of the priesthood are intimately connected to the reputation and status of the church and, more importantly, to the reputation and credibility of the church's teaching office. If its reputation is sullied, the credibility of its teaching and prophetic roles will be diminished. From this perspective, the crimes and sins of priests and bishops abusing teenagers and children created a daunting challenge to the church's authority and credibility.

The clergy abuse scandal also threatened the structures of order and power that are supported by the discipline and law of mandatory celibacy. Church officials know instinctively that the exercise of authority over celibate priests is quite different—and less difficult—than is the exercise of authority over married priests. Without the emotional and affective support of wife and children, the celibate priest's psychic investment in "holy mother church" is necessarily deep and pervasive. He is, on a number of levels, married to the church. Neither husband nor father, his identity is especially rooted in his role of celibate priest. Without the humanizing and humbling challenges of marriage and parenthood, the negative elements now recognized in clerical culture as manifestations of clericalism are fostered and nourished.

Although exact figures remain unclear, it is estimated that approximately two hundred Latin rite Catholic priests minister as married men in the U.S. These married priests are converts from Episcopal and Protestant denominations who believe, often because of the ordination of women in their respective churches, that they are called to full communion with Roman Catholicism. While also "married" to the church, the spiritual sinews of their psychic lives binding them to mother church are less fibrous, less dense. They may indeed be as clerical as their celibate colleagues, but overall the inescapable vulnerability and accountability inherent to the married state adds another human dimension to their experience of life and ministry. As their administrators, bishops must cope with an added layer of complexity in shepherding the shepherds—especially in making pastoral assignments and in dealing both administratively and pastorally with the inevitable family and marital difficulties that are bound to arise in at least some of the lives of married clergy.

While the abuse of children and minors cannot be directly linked to celibacy—the vast majority of abusers are married men—when the possible structural factors of the abuse scandal are explored, the issue of mandatory celibacy soon becomes central. It is still unknown from a proportional perspective whether abuse of minors and children is more, the same, or less prevalent among celibate clergy than among married men. It is a question that many church leaders shy away from. They fear the answer may imply that mandatory celibacy isn't working. While many believe today that it isn't, church authorities insist that it is working. They claim that where celibacy appears to be in disarray, it is due primarily to lack of fidelity to prayer and/or to moral weakness. To the extent that church officials are fearful of any questioning of mandatory celibacy, it explains the Vatican's apparent unwillingness to address the widespread disregard of priestly celibacy commonly observed in numerous Latin American and African countries. European and North American missionaries report that more than half the priests in these countries live in open relationships with women—relationships that for the most part are accepted by their parishioners and the wider community.

Why is such open disregard for the discipline and law of celibacy tolerated by the Vatican? Two explanations, I believe, are probable. First, the extent of these relationships is such that to enforce mandatory celibacy might lead to widespread resignations from the priesthood resulting in sacramental and pastoral crises in areas of the Catholic world already experiencing serious shortages of priestly ministry. Second, such an enforcement of celibacy would bring the issue to the attention of the wider Catholic world and give support to the growing contention that mandatory celibacy, as distinct from freely chosen celibacy, simply isn't working.

Furthermore, attention to widespread public disregard for celibacy in numerous cultures might raise the long-standing question relating to the church's attempt to mandate a charism (a term referring to a gift of the Spirit, such as the aptitude for preaching, teaching, and celibacy, given to an individual for the good of the community of believers). If celibacy is a gift of the Spirit given to some—and it would seem, relatively few—members of the faithful, how can the church claim that this gift is given to each and every candidate for the priesthood? Does the church really have this kind of influence with God? Did the priests, bishops, and popes of the first millennium of Christianity who were married refuse this gift? Are married Catholic priests of the Eastern churches in communion with Rome unaware of their charism for celibacy? Is the Latin rite more favored by God in the granting of charisms than the Eastern churches who are in full communion with the bishop of Rome?

A look back to the first centuries of the church may prove surprising to some believers. Both Pope Sixtus I (c. 116–125) and Pope Damasus I (366–384) were sons of priests. And Pope Saint Anastasius I (395–401) was the father of Pope Saint Innocent I (401–417). Furthermore, Pope Saint Hormisdas (514–523) was the father of Pope Saint Silverius (536–537) although his son did not succeed him directly. Approximately a dozen popes were sons of priests in the first millennium. Adrian II (867–872) was the last married pope but Pope John XV (985–986) was the son of a priest. If mandatory celibacy were in place then, we would have inherited a very different papal lineage, and the church would never have had the benefit of a number of saintly bishops, pastors, and preachers. Is there some reason why God cannot call now—as God apparently did for the first thousand years of the church—individuals to both the sacrament of orders and the sacrament of marriage? Does the church have the right to say to candidates for the Latin rite priesthood that they may not respond to the vocation of marriage? Does the church mean to claim the wisdom to know to whom God has given the vocation of marriage and to whom God has not given this calling?

More than twenty thousand priests in the U.S. alone have left the active ministry, many if not most, in order to marry. Listening to their stories we learn they believe they are called both to priesthood and marriage. Is it right for the church to insist that the Spirit of God would not do such a thing, even though the Spirit apparently did so for centuries? Has not the church given more weight and dignity to celibacy than to the sacrament of marriage? And if celibacy is presented, as it often is, as a spiritual discipline that candidates for the priesthood must "freely" accept in order to be ordained, then how explain the precedence given to a discipline, no matter how noble, over a sacrament of the church?

The Clergy Vocation Crisis

U.S. Catholics have watched with concern and surprise as the number of priests dropped a staggering 40 percent in the last

decades of the twentieth century; a figure exceeded by an even
greater decline in the number of candidates preparing for the
priesthood. The average age of the ordained moves steadily up into
the sixties, with more priests currently in their nineties than under
thirty-five. All this while the American Catholic population rose
during the same period to an all time high of sixty-seven million.
Approximately one out of five American parishes is without a resi-
dent pastor while one half of the world's Catholic parishes worship
without a priest—at least on most Sundays. With exceptions in
scattered parts of the world, church authorities in Western Europe,
North America, and most countries in Latin America, Africa, and
Asia cope as best they can with the ever-growing priest shortage
and the concomitant sacramental crisis.

Although most theologians and biblical scholars find no doctrinal or scriptural reasons prohibiting the ordination of women,
Pope John Paul II has spoken definitively that it is not possible for
the church to ordain women as priests. In light of this teaching,
many Catholics ask what is keeping the church from ordaining
women to the diaconate? In spite of some denials, there is both
historical precedent and wide scholarly support for ordaining
women as deacons. Perhaps church authorities fear that ordaining
women deacons would fuel the still vibrant movement for the ordination of women to the priesthood. The issue of mandated celibacy for diocesan priests (at least in theory, religious order priests
believe they are called by charism both to priesthood and to celibate life in community or shared apostolic ministry) and the barring of women from the priesthood remain in the minds of many
Catholics significant factors in the vocation crisis. Still another
factor deserves consideration.

Demographic research indicates that the average number of
children in a Catholic family is 1.8—the very same number of
children per household in the U.S. population as a whole. With
two children or less, it is likely that most Catholic households will
have but one son. Concern for the family name alone might dis-
suade Catholic parents from encouraging their son from pursuing

studies for the priesthood. Furthermore, a study commissioned by the U.S. Catholic bishops found that two-thirds of Catholic parents would disagree or strongly disagree with the following statement: "I would encourage a son or daughter who showed interest in the priesthood or religious life." A half century ago, the majority of Catholic parents would have taken pride in a son or daughter who felt called to the priesthood or religious life. The significant decline in the average number of children in Catholic families when linked with the startling change in parents' attitude toward their children's possible interest in a religious vocation augurs poorly for any surge in candidates for the priesthood or religious life.

In addition to the factors we have already mentioned, the very social and economic success of American Catholics is pertinent. Vocations were abundant when Catholics in the U.S. were mostly immigrant and ethnic. Working class parents understood that the convent and seminary would provide an education for their children the likes of which they could not afford. Add to this practical consideration the status and dignity attached to religious vocations in the middle of the twentieth century and, from a human perspective alone, it is not surprising that parental encouragement and family support were abundant. Fifty years later, Catholic parents are generally well educated, often holding undergraduate and postgraduate degrees. The explosion in the number of vocational choices now available for their children and enjoying the financial means to pursue them have played major roles in the current dearth of religious vocations. For numerous Catholic students and young adults, priesthood and religious life aren't even "on their screen," to use a cyberspace idiom. When the damage to the image and status of the priesthood caused by the sexual abuse scandal is factored in, the immediate future is abysmal.

Still, the only action taken by many bishops in the face of this ministerial crisis is to call for prayers for vocations and more active recruiting. There is little recognition from church authorities that the present vocation crisis is—to a considerable extent—a crisis aided and abetted by the institutional church itself.

Clergy Abuse

This sad, seemingly endless tragedy has scarred thousands of young, innocent victims and at the same time scarred to the point of profound disfigurement the credibility of the nation's Catholic bishops. The long collective cry of lament of the last decades of the twentieth century promises to be heard well into the first decades of the twenty-first century if not beyond. The scandal and its equally scandalous bungling by numerous bishops and their attorneys have unveiled, as we saw in chapter 1, serious issues relating to structure and governance. For many, however, the scandal raised afresh the complexity, even the mystery, of human behavior.

Since the abuse scandals became front-page news in the 1980s, countless Catholics and others have been asking how men who have spent years in seminary formation studying Scripture, ethics, and theology could bring themselves to sexually exploit children and teens and not at the same time be driven mad with guilt and remorse? Not only do a number of priest abusers apparently feel little or no guilt about their actions, they often appear self-absorbed, even narcissistic. Elsewhere I cited John Cornwell's report in his book *Breaking Faith: The Pope, the People, and the Fate of Catholicism* of a British priest who unabashedly describes his lust for a young college student at the school where he ministered as chaplain. This extraordinary window on the inner working of a priest abuser's erotic desire merits a second telling:

> Not long before he died, one of my close priest friends who had a position of responsibility as chaplain in a Catholic residential college told me on his sixty-ninth birthday that he was currently attempting to seduce an eighteen-year-old male student into a sexual liaison. Wise and evidently good in countless ways, he was a stirring preacher and a man who loved his priesthood, but I came to see that his life was profoundly dislocated. I realized that although I had been acquainted with him for twenty-five years, I hardly knew him at all. He said, "I'm convinced that I cannot become fully human until I've had sexual relations with this young man." At

one point he said, "Oh, the body is just a playground; it's the soul that matters."

Clearly, this is but one priest's almost casual observation of his carnal desire for a young man to a writer he knew as a friend. Still, it may shed some light on the question that continues to puzzle many: how can men well educated in their faith, who preach the word of God, who are respected as wise pastors, think— and behave—as literally thousands of priests have done?

The context is telling. A Catholic chaplain in his seventieth year of age ministers at a residential college. Cornwell informs us the priest is a "stirring preacher and a man who loved his priesthood." Somehow this senior chaplain has reconciled his sexual desire and his determination to bring it to fulfillment with his role and identity as a priest. He did not say to Cornwell that he had become obsessed with a young man and that he was aware of the incongruity and inappropriateness of his sexual longing. If he had, then we might assume that he was struggling to remain chaste, that he understood this strong attraction as a temptation that needed to be resisted. But there was none of this. He spoke openly to Cornwell without apparent embarrassment or shame not only about his desire but his current attempts to seduce the student.

There is no hint that the priest had been surprised by his keen attraction to the young man or that if he acted upon this attraction he would have been betraying his role of chaplain to foster the spiritual lives of the students in his pastoral care. Nor is there a hint that he perceives any personal harm to the young man in question, that he knows he is contradicting the moral teaching of the church and the moral sensitivity, if not the laws, of society itself. "Oh, the body is just a playground;" he says, "it's the soul that matters." There is indeed a dimension of play in human sexuality, but sexuality's power both to exalt the human spirit and to subvert the life of the soul is one of the great lessons of spiritual and religious wisdom.

Moreover, our chaplain's sexual quest is presented to Cornwell as a compelling drive for human fulfillment. "I'm convinced that I cannot become fully human until I've had sexual relations with this young man." The priest gives the impression he is on a noble venture to become integrated, to become fully human. Did he really believe that he had a moral imperative to pursue his sexual conquest of this eighteen-year-old student? The chaplain's disturbing almost "by the way" acknowledgment of his sexual longing, on face value, does lead to this conclusion—he really believed he was on a spiritual quest!

What is to be made of this revealing admission? Some reasonable assumptions follow: this is not the first young man to fall under the eye of the chaplain. How many previous pursuits and seductions were there? Were they mostly men his own age? Were they mostly younger adults, even students? Would the chaplain's sexual history reveal attitudes and patterns of behavior that would help church authorities to understand the etiology and nature of the current sexual abuse cases? John Cornwell's brief but important report of his friend's sexual longing for a young man leaves us with unsettling questions, but it also suggests two possible scenarios that in turn may lead to some understanding.

Scenario I. I know priests who while in the seminary devoted a good number of hours each day to reading Greek and Latin classical authors—in Greek and Latin. With but a hint of intellectual superiority, they slyly let it be known that they were reading classical erotica: the escapades, adventures, and seductions of youth, especially boys, by men of ancient Greece and Rome recorded in the poetry and plays of that era. The penchant for man-boy love in ancient Greece has been well documented by Kenneth Dover in his 1978 study *Greek Homosexuality*. In his 1988 book *The Greeks and Their Legacy*, Dover asserts that Greeks "regarded homosexual desire as natural, normal, and universal." Seminarians, in particular gay seminarians, reading the likes of Sophocles, Catullus, Euripides, and others may perceive pederasty as did Cornwell's elderly college chaplain.

Since man-boy love was acclaimed and celebrated by major poets and writers of antiquity—Plato proposed that boys live together and be made available to serve the sexual needs of different men—have clergy and other men attracted to youth reasoned that only narrow-minded bourgeoisie would object to older men turning to the glorified youth of their day for sensual gratification? For in these seductions mature adults initiated the gifted and chosen youth not only into the pleasures of sexual intimacy, they instructed them in the disciplined pursuit of rhetorical skills, knowledge, and wisdom. Is it not possible that priests schooled in the classics drew on their classical education to justify sexual contact with teenagers? Their knowledge of the sexual habits and practices of ancient poets and writers may also have contributed to the air of superiority, both intellectual and aesthetic, that can be sensed in the attitudes and poses of some priest abusers. Since the majority of priests ordained before Vatican II had considerable familiarity with the classics, might there not be a connection? The seminarians, it should be noted, who prided themselves in reading classical authors writing about the joys and pleasures of sex with youth were eventually ordained. Each has been accused of sexual misconduct with minors.

Scenario II. Between 1880 and 1930 a literary genre surfaced in England that is disturbingly prescient of the current abuse crisis. I draw here on Ellis Hanson's 1997 book *Decadence and Catholicism* in which the author recounts that during this roughly fifty-year period there was a proliferation of priest-acolyte narratives and poetry that centered on the loves—and lust—of both Anglican and Catholic priests for their acolytes. At the center of this genre is John Francis Bloxam's story "The Priest and the Acolyte" in which a young priest falls in love with his fourteen-year-old acolyte. In Hanson's words

> They become lovers, inspiring each other to new heights of spiritual perfection. Unfortunately, they are discovered together in a compromising situation by the rector. Ronald [the priest] defends the purity and beauty of their love, but eventually, in a highly melodramatic and romantic gesture, man and boy commit suicide together in a ritual that imitates the Mass.

We are led to believe there is something noble, even sacred, in the spiritual and physical bonding of these lovers.

Similar cords of spirit and flesh are found in Edmund John's 1913 poem "The Acolyte." In the lines below we "hear" the silent gasp of a priest caught off guard by the sudden pull of an attraction both spiritual and carnal:

> Then through the monkish hymn
> A strange note and a piercing sweetness ran;
> And a young priest, who saw thee, clutched his beads,
> And grew all pale as from the organ reeds
> Peeled once again the poignant pipes of Pan.

Both Edmund John and John Francis Bloxam, in light of Hanson's analysis, provide a glimpse of the common theme running through the narratives and poetry of this genre—"[the] contesting [of] conventional beliefs about the relationship between sexuality and religious experience" *(Decadence and Catholicism)*. This contesting, I propose, coupled with the sexual revolution of the 1960s and beyond are major causal factors influencing the seductions of John Cornwell's friend and countless other priests. There is something to be learned from this proliferation of priest-acolyte narratives and poetry. They certainly romanticized and spiritualized man-boy sexual relationships and in doing so linked the sexual ambiguity of priests to the sensual aesthetics of ecclesial ritual. Modern psychology has made clear what mystics and the world's major religious traditions have known for centuries—there exists an intimate intertwining between the spiritual and the sensual. Do the priest-acolyte tales of a century ago have something to say to us about the present abuse scandal? Do these narratives and poems in turn draw on the plays and poems of the classical period? Are we witnessing a variation on a sexual drama that has been played out in turn from antiquity through the Middle Ages, the post-Reformation period, the Victorian era, down to our own time? Do we dare ask these questions?

The Uses of Fear

Behind and underneath the tensions and hostilities of the post-conciliar cultural wars lay a sea of fear. "Progressive" Catholics who embrace the council's vision of renewal fear the consequences of being labeled "liberal," convinced—I believe correctly—they are really the centrists of the post-Vatican II church. They fear the church's growing centralization that threatens the identity and autonomy of the local church. They fear the promised renewal of the council is being betrayed by the fears of powerful and high placed church authorities who believe the council was a terrible mistake. They fear the threatened (and in many parts of the U.S. and beyond, already realized) loss of the Eucharist due to the shrinking ranks of the priesthood. And they fear the loss of hope they perceive in the eyes of their families, fellow parishioners, and their pastoral leaders.

Large numbers of Catholics who consider themselves neither progressive nor conservative fear the church is growing ever more out of touch with the daily, ordinary challenges of their lives. They fear the loss of the church's prophetic voice as society at large, and Catholics themselves question the credibility of the bishops. For the most part untroubled by the mounting tensions between progressives and conservatives, they fear for the future of their once vital parish and lament the overall quality of their parish's liturgical life. They worry about the future of their parish school and the health of their overworked pastor. If not quite as fearful as their progressive and conservative fellow Catholics, they sense that serious challenges confront the church of their ancestors and the church of their youth.

Conservative Catholics fear the loss of ecclesial order, conformity, grandeur, and mystery that remains firmly lodged in their collective memories. They fear the compromising of ecclesiastical authority, and a creeping democratization of the church. They fear the blurring of lines between the clergy and laity and the softer, more pliable understandings of ecclesiastical hierarchy suggested by the council. They fear criticism of patriarchy and the emerging feminism in both society and church. They fear charisms freely given by the Spirit that are not under the explicit control of the institutional church. They fear theologians who do not limit their research and writing to the shoring up of curial and papal teachings and pronouncements. And perhaps their greatest fear is the loss of fear itself.

Without question, a hallmark of the post-conciliar church is a renewed emphasis on the freedom and dignity of the people of God rather than on the obligations of a fundamentally passive laity. Depending on one's ecclesiology, this is either cause for rejoicing or for profound concern. Denying neither the obligations nor the responsibilities of the baptized, the council echoed the gospel's ringing endorsement of spiritual freedom.

> Blessed be the Lord, the God of Israel;
> he has come to his people and set them free . . .
> This was the oath he swore to our father Abraham:
> to set us free from the hands of our enemies,
> free to worship him without fear,
> holy and righteous in his sight
>   all the days of our life (Luke 1:68, 73-75).

In the pre-conciliar church fear was in the ascendancy over freedom, in particular, the fear of sin and especially the fear of eternal punishment in hell. The one, great religious task was to "save one's soul," to avoid the unending pains of hell and to achieve everlasting bliss with God and the communion of saints in the heavenly mansions prepared for us. Since the council, freedom is in the ascendancy over fear, in particular, the freedom to choose faithful, mature discipleship as a follower of Jesus the Christ in the grace and power of the Holy Spirit.

Older Catholics look back on their religious upbringing with both nostalgia and considerable anger. For out of paternal concern for their spiritual welfare, the shepherds of the church feared to trust their maturity as adult believers. They see now the bishops' concern and fear that they would not have a strong enough faith to do what was necessary and essential to remain on the path to salvation. Consider some of the signs of their shepherds' fear. Prayer remains a cornerstone of the spiritual life and of discipleship. But the gospel obligation to lead prayerful lives was deemed to be insufficient. Out of fear of the faithfuls' human weakness, the shepherds declared it was a sin not to pray. Fearful that believers would not pray unless motivated to avoid sin, church authorities taught it was a sin to miss saying one's morning prayers or night prayers. Fear of sin, it was reasoned, would motivate believers to do what was right and necessary—to pray. And because the celebration of the Eucharist is likewise essential for maintaining one's communion with God and the people of God, the church taught and still teaches that a Catholic sins gravely if he or she misses Mass on Sundays without a sufficient reason such as illness or when travelling. Without this motivation to avoid serious sin and the concomitant fear of damnation, it was thought that Catholics would simply miss Mass regularly. And because it is essential for ordained clergy to be men of prayer, the obligation to pray the Liturgy of the Hours (the daily prayers of the breviary) carried the weight of serious sin if not completed as prescribed. And because ascetical practices are part of the discipline of discipleship, it was the church's long standing practice to teach that it was seriously sinful to eat meat on Friday.

Out of fear of human weakness among other motives, church authorities used the threat of sin to motivate people to "practice their faith." No matter how well intentioned, the multiplication of sin to insure external compliance with church teaching and church law lays bare the misguided paternalism of feudal lords. How do we explain the uses of fear that fostered if not created what has come to be known as "Catholic guilt?" Only immature and misguided faith would embrace such tactics.

Bishop Heaps gets to the heart of the matter: "[W]hat sort of a church did we have when the motive for worship or for morality was fear? How does it all fit in with a relationship of love of God, a desire to be one with Christ, a longing for his Kingdom of justice, love and peace to come?" *(A Love That Dares to Question)*. Obviously, Catholics imagined God before the council as loving parent, but the controlling image, sustained and reinforced by a controlling paternalism, was God as judge. Alienation from God through misuse of human freedom—and the concomitant alienation from the communion of believers—is the great human tragedy. It is indeed to be feared. But as the church teaches, we are saved by the freely bestowed redeeming grace of Jesus the Christ in the power of the Holy Spirit. In Christ fear is transformed into trust, trust in the enduring presence of the Spirit who has promised never to abandon God's holy people.

Fear and the Galileo Affair

Ancient history to some, the Galileo affair raises questions the church would like to see put to rest since John Paul II's address to the Pontifical Academy of Sciences in October 1992. The pope acknowledged the church was wrong to have condemned Galileo for holding to his position that the earth was not the center of the universe (the geocentric position supported by a literal reading of Genesis), but that it moved about the sun (the heliocentric model of the cosmos). It is both significant and important that the pope admitted the error. Still, important lessons relevant to the church's present crisis can be drawn from the church's condemnation of Galileo.

Born in Pisa in 1564, Galileo Galilei distinguished himself as a philosopher, astronomer, and mathematician. Building on the theoretical foundations of Nicolas Copernicus's heliocentric model, Galileo with the aid of his telescope confirmed the inadequacy of the geocentric model as proposed by Scripture and affirmed by such thinkers as Plato and Aristotle. Aware that his research would likely place him under the suspicion of the Inquisition, Galileo, unlike Copernicus who waited until he was close to death before publishing his findings, nevertheless moved forward cautiously. How else could he have proceeded with his work? The monk and philosopher Girordano Bruno had been burned at the stake in 1600 for holding, among other things, to the Copernican theory. Galileo was spared the stake, but lived the last years of his life under house arrest for his audacious contention.

Jacques Maritain, in his book *On the Church of Christ*, notes that Galileo underwent four different interrogations by the judges of the Holy Office—all under threat of torture. When he finally brought himself to abjure his heliocentric theory in the presence of his judges, Galileo did so on his knees with his hand on a Bible. Maritain comments, "With regard to the judges of the Holy Office, I do not see another term than that of *abuse of power*. . . . In the verdict of condemnation [of Galileo] they declared that the opinion of Copernicus had been *defined* 'contrary to the Holy Scriptures.' Defined by whom?" Maritain asks, "By the Church, by the Pope speaking *ex cathedra*? Not at all. Defined by them alone, fallible men."

Without question, the church's understanding of biblical inspiration and biblical scholarship was quite different in Galileo's day from the council's Dogmatic Constitution on Divine Revelation. Still, Maritain's critique of Galileo's condemnation is striking in the sharpness of its tone. Perhaps it was Maritain's strong criticism of Galileo's condemnation that nudged the church to make a formal admission that it had erred. Astronomer James Orgren in his essay "Copernicus, Galileo, and the Catholic Church, Then and Now," writes, "The pope [John Paul II] said that seventeenth-century theologians had erred in assuming that the 'literal sense of Sacred Scripture' explained the physical world. He acknowledged that Galileo had developed better rules for scriptural interpretation than the theologians of the time. He also said it was an important matter to understand in case of future conflicts between religion and science. Finally, he acknowledged that the Inquisition had wronged Galileo."

The church's response to scientific research that threatens its understanding of the faith in the twenty-first century is, at least in one respect, similar to the church's response to the Galileo

affair: it forbids even discussion of such research as well as theological and ethical issues and church disciplines (such as optional
celibacy for diocesan priests) previously declared out of bounds.
The will to silence (and punish) what appears to be opposition to
or dissent from entrenched church teaching is often successful in
the short run, leaving deep scars on the lives and careers of faithful Catholics who dared to enter into the dangerous waters of
honest research. In the long run, however, it fails, leaving the
church looking defensive and still hostile to academic freedom.
Does the institutional church really believe it has nothing to fear
from the truth, scientific or otherwise?

A number of other questions arise from the Galileo affair.
Galileo's heliocentric model was condemned by the church in
1633. But his theory became more and more the accepted model
as ongoing research confirmed its veracity. The church came to
know it had erred and in 1757 removed from the Index of forbidden books previously proscribed works teaching the mobility
of the earth around the sun, but it wasn't until 1822 that the
books of Copernicus and Galileo were removed. Why the delay?
And why did it take until the pontificate of John Paul II for the
church to acknowledge publicly and officially that it had it been
wrong to condemn the work of Galileo, and by implication, other
scientists like Nicolas Copernicus, Johann Kepler, and Giordano
Bruno?

The pre-modern worldview of Galileo's era explains to a considerable degree why the Inquisition and Pope Urban VIII felt
compelled to take action against him. But continued scientific research into the modern era made it clear centuries before John
Paul lifted the formal sanctions against him that Galileo was correct. However, fear that the authority and power of the church
might be diminished prompted high-ranking church authorities to
let the injustices of the Galileo affair remain unaddressed for hundreds of years. It was the same fear that prompted bishops to move
abusing priests from one unsuspecting parish to another and in
some cases from one diocese to another. It was the same fear that

motivated dioceses to demand confidentiality agreements when settlements were reached with abuse victims and their families. It was the same fear that directed diocesan attorneys to employ hardball tactics in depositions with victims of clergy abuse.

What was first feared by the church as a threat to the integrity of the faith came to be seen as no threat at all. But in the meantime—such human suffering! Commemorating the centenary of Albert Einstein's birth in November 1979, John Paul II addressed the Pontifical Academy of Sciences and admitted that Galileo suffered unjustly at the hands of the church. The pope went on to praise Galileo for his authentic religious spirit and for the integrity of his views relating to science and religion. Both in 1979 and later in 1992 when John Paul II again spoke to the members of the Pontifical Academy of Sciences, he acknowledged that the church had erred in the condemnation of Galileo. What the pope knew to be true popes for generations before him had known to be true. But John Paul's predecessors had remained silent.

The long delay to set the record straight is troubling to believers of the twentieth and twenty-first centuries. Where was the church's "grace of self-doubt"—at least in matters of science? Where was the humility to admit what the world knew? Where was the witness to the truth from a church that proclaims to be the bearer of the Truth? When fear smothers courage, when status and power trump integrity and pastoral care, we feel the shaking of the church's foundations. When the welfare of the institutional church takes precedence over the welfare of God's people and fidelity to the gospel, we find ourselves at the very borders of idolatry.

There are times when love for the church requires that the people of God dare to question certain non-dogmatic, non-revealed teachings and issues the hierarchy holds untouchable. The faithful have both the right and obligation to question structures, practices, and disciplines that no longer serve the pastoral needs of the church nor its mission.

CHAPTER FOUR

FAITH THAT DARES TO SPEAK

If the church does not subject itself to the judgment which is pronounced by the church, it becomes idolatrous towards itself. Such idolatry is its permanent temptation. . . . A church which tries to exclude itself from such a judgment loses its right to judge the world and is rightly judged by the world. This is the tragedy of the Roman Catholic Church.

—Paul Tillich

We will not understand the meaning of prophetic imagination unless we see the connection between the *religion of static triumphalism* and the *politics of oppression and exploitation*.

—Walter Brueggemann

THE FEELING GROWS among U.S. Catholics that things will never be the same. Clergy sexual abuse, the abuse of ecclesiastical power, and the church's financial scandals have awakened believers from a long, indolent slumber to a fresh comprehension of their dignity as God's people—and to a clear conviction that the church's current way of doing business just isn't working. They concede that the vision and pastoral sensitivity of the next pope will be perhaps the most critical factor determining the immediate future of the church, but they also sense that their role, the role of the laity, will likewise be a major determining factor. Awake and alert to their post-conciliar status and responsibilities, they become visibly angry when prelates declare that it is time to get beyond the sexual, financial, and fiduciary scandals and settle back into the way things were.

It appears that the bishops think they have turned the corner on the current hard times because they are implementing comprehensive policies and norms for dealing with abuse reports, are settling to the best of their abilities and diocesan resources the civil lawsuits against local churches, and in some dioceses meeting personally with abuse victims. But the specter of reform sends chills down the bishops' spines. From their perspective, there is no need for structural reform or for greater lay involvement in church governance. Their collective attitude falls along the following lines. There was a problem and after some serious initial missteps we have regained our footing and now it is time to move on. Meaning that it is time to move back to the relative calm of the years before Lafayette, Fall River, and Boston became the epicenters of the clergy abuse scandals.

As a group, the U.S. bishops dismiss as pessimistic and overwrought Peter Steinfel's sobering beginning to his book *A People Adrift*, "Today the Roman Catholic Church in the United States is on the verge of either an irreversible decline or a thoroughgoing transformation." His book provides ample evidence for such a declaration. In *The Coming Catholic Church*, David Gibson treats with candor and clarity the depth and breadth of the present crisis. Both books make clear that the present troubles go well beyond the sexual exploitation of children and minors. Each points to the important role the laity must play as the church comes to grip with the present situation. It is their moment to step forward and to speak bravely.

A Voice from Mexico

While it remains important, even critical, for the laity to raise their voices and to have their voices heard by church officials, the voice of a Mexican Carmelite priest may well inspire laity, priests, and vowed religious to engage in daring speech. Fr. Camilo Macisse, until recently the superior general of the Discalced Carmelites, also served until 2000 as president of the Union of Superiors General, the organization of male religious who lead and govern their respective orders and congregations. As president of the USG, Macisse had an up-close look at the culture of the Roman curia. In a candid and compelling essay published in the November 23, 2003, issue of *The Tablet*, he decried the violence he observed and felt while working closely with Vatican officials.

Macisse defines violence as the application of physical, moral, or psychological force to impose or coerce. By definition, violence is inimical to the gospel of peace and justice preached by Jesus. Yet the church has employed violence to resolve conflicts which inevitably arise "between the hierarchy and the grass roots, between the institutional and charismatic dimensions of the church, between traditional and novel understandings of the faith, [between] theologians and the teaching authority, and [between] church and society." The use of violence, Macisse sadly notes, has been a part of the culture of church authority down through the ages. While no longer employing physical violence, the church continues to use moral and psychological forms of violence. "I have had intimate knowledge of this violence, above all as exercised by a number of Roman departments. It comes in many forms."

Macisse's litany of examples of church violence begins with centralism, the concentration of decision-making powers in church authorities far removed from the circumstances and everyday lives of believers. "[I]t is a way of treating believers at all levels, from bishops' conferences to groups of lay people, as children in need of protection who must be disciplined according to short-sighted criteria."

Another form of violence, that of patriarchal authoritarianism, surfaced when the church's document on enclosure for contemplative women religious, *Verbi Sponsa*, was issued without consulting any of the forty-nine associations or federations of Discalced Carmelites. "[O]nly the opinion of a small number of traditionalist convents was sought," reports Macisse. "The resulting legislation, drawn up by men whose knowledge of female religious life is entirely theoretical, demands of women what it does not demand of men, and is an example of the discriminatory violence directed at consecrated contemplative women. As in former times, they are viewed as children incapable of fidelity to their cloistered identity without male supervision." Moreover, when Catholics are reported to the Congregation for the Doctrine of the faith for suspected error or heresy, their accuser or accusers are guaranteed anonymity. The accused may not present witnesses to testify on their behalf. Nor are those making accusations encouraged to first take their concerns to those whom they are reporting, as the gospel encourages. "[C]urial officials . . . cloak themselves in a sacred power. They cannot be accused of slander and defamation. They demand blind obedience, and insist that such matters fall under the 'exclusive competence of the Holy See.'" We have come a long way from the Inquisition, the use of torture, the imposition of the death penalty, the Index of forbidden books, but still we have miles to go.

Not long ago I sat at dinner with a European priest and scholar who had just undergone an investigation by the Congregation for the Doctrine of the Faith. He was found to be innocent of the charge of heresy but the pain and suffering of his ordeal—the disillusionment, the strain on his health, the crushing discouragement rising up from the well-grounded suspicion that some of his own colleagues had reported him was evident. Did this eminent scholar know Camilo Macisse? Whether they had ever met I don't know. But they had much in common. As I listened to his story, there was no doubt about it—we have miles to go.

Above all, Macisse insists the church needs an attitude of dialogue where individuals listen respectfully and discern the truth in the light of the gospel. His experience as a major superior of religious men and his first-hand knowledge of the culture of the curia gained while president of the Union of Superiors General give weight to his cry for renewal and reform. Father Macisse dared to speak. Though calling for that which the Second Vatican Council itself called for, he knows full well his voice will not be welcomed in numerous corners of the church nor in the halls and offices of the Roman curia. For his efforts he may well come to know virtual exile. May he not stand alone.

Voices from Exile

Since the council's close in the fall of 1965, Catholics familiar with its fundamental teachings have carried in their hearts a vision of what a renewed church might be like. Aware now that the church is the communion of the baptized first and foremost, the long-standing over-identification of the church with its institutional dimension has been, at least in theory, corrected. Catholics now understood the true essence of the church as never before. No longer passive members of the church, they have come to appreciate their rightful place in the household of God. With this fresh insight into the nature of the church came hope and a sense of being "at home" in the church. There was a palpable sense of joy and vitality among Catholics in the years immediately following Vatican II. But it didn't last as powerful church authorities began to undermine the council's dramatic and liberating reforms. Control over almost every aspect of church life was reclaimed by the Vatican leaving diocesan bishops in the position of branch managers and the lower ranks of the clergy along with their parishioners frustrated and resentful. For many among the laity, vowed religious, and clergy, the retrenchment was a disheartening betrayal of the council. Their voices, in the words of Walter Brueggemann, were "vetoed and nullified and canceled so that [they] had no say in the future of the community or of [their] own lives" (The Prophetic Imagination). They found themselves decidedly not "at home" in their church. It was as if they were in exile.

Unlike the Israelites, who suffered the Babylonian exile and took strength and hope from the prophet Isaiah's promise of deliverance, they hear no words of comfort, no words of encouragement. Instead of Second Isaiah's rousing: "Fear not, I am with you; / be not dismayed; I am your God. / I will strengthen you and help you. . . ." (Isa 41:10), they remember instead the words of Lamentations, "The youths carry the millstones, / boys stagger under their loads of wood; . . . / The joy of our hearts has ceased, our dance has turned into mourning" (5:13, 15). Victims of clergy sexual abuse carry the millstones of shame and betrayal, their loads weighted down with the denial and dismissal that often greeted their reports to church authorities. Word continues to spread of bishops who bully their priests and people, who fail to listen, who fail to lead. The hearts of the faithful no longer leap, let alone dance, with joy. If the homeless are in a sense exiles in place, young girls discouraged still in some parishes from serving at the altar suffer exile. Women who remain well removed for the most part from key positions of leadership in the church suffer exile. The divorced who for various reasons cannot enter into the process necessary to obtain declarations of nullity suffer exile. Priests who felt called to the intimacy of the sacrament of marriage suffer exile. Committed gay and lesbian Catholics suffer the exile of their "disordered conditions." Laity whose love for the church prompts them to ask questions and seek information without appropriate response from their bishops suffer exile. For exiles in place it remains a bitter time—a time for grief and lament.

Cries of Lament

As a former seminary rector and vicar for clergy and religious, I am often asked how I think today's priests are coping in light of the abuse scandal, their diminished status in the eyes of many, and their own disappointment, sometimes bitter, with the stalled reforms of Vatican II. Polarized, demoralized, fearful, resentful, they are. But they are also hardworking, persevering, faithful, and, in growing numbers, courageous.

The evening before I sat down to write these paragraphs, I met for dinner with four priests in a rustic restaurant called the Gamekeeper's Taverne. We were hardly outdoorsmen, much less gamekeepers, but we were faith-keepers and, in spite of our own discouragement, servants of the faithful working hard to keep their courage high and their hope alive. But yesterday evening, truth be told, we gathered for company and a good meal in order to keep our own courage high and our own hope alive. I glanced around the table and looked into the eyes of men who had served long and well. Any observer would have seen in their eyes intelligence, a sense of humor, and fidelity. Unmistakably, though, there were hints of resignation, fatigue, and discouragement. Not surprisingly, we discussed the church's leadership crisis and the priesthood's crisis. Our conversation made it clear we were men without illusions. Each of us knew the clerical system and how it worked. Just beneath the surface of our reflections, I sensed a common thread of lament. We were men who were grieving and the issues on the table were the same issues being addressed in the private conversations of priests from coast to coast—the future of the church, the emerging role of the laity, the dearth of episcopal leadership, and the changing face of ministry.

As the evening wore on, the substance and tone of our conversation confirmed my earlier impression that priests are grieving. To be sure, some are grieving the imagined halcyon days of Bing Crosby playing Fr. Chuck O'Malley in *Going My Way* and *The Bells of St. Mary* when the status and authority of the priest was unquestioned. Most, I believe, are grieving the aborted promise and vision of the council. They are grieving the terrible wounds inflicted by significant numbers of their brother priests, wounds that were again and again compounded by bishops and other church officials who feared scandal and the loss of the clergy's reputation that, in turn, threatened their own credibility and power. They are grieving the complete breakdown of honest dialogue between bishops and priests. Almost all grieve the current ministerial crisis— especially the growing, forced fasting from Eucharist caused by the shortage of priests—and the future of the priesthood. They share in the grief and anguish of women who feel they remain second class members of the church. Many grieve the loneliness inherent in celibacy and the hierarchy's unwillingness even to discuss the issue of mandatory celibacy. Others grieve the children they never fathered and the wife they never married. Their grief, to be sure, is mixed with the deep joy they find in presiding at Eucharist, in preaching, in ministering to their congregations. At least for the present, lament has the upper hand.

The grieving of priests, however, pales when we turn to the victims of clergy sexual abuse. Their cry of lament, and the cry of their parents, siblings, and friends bind them to the biblical Rachel and all who weep for the wronged children of the world. "In Ramah is heard the sound of moaning, / of bitter weeping! / Rachel mourns her children," . . . (Jer 31:15). The months that followed the eruption of the John Geoghan scandal in early January 2002 have been dubbed by various writers as the *long Lent*. And it isn't over yet. Until the light rays of resurrection finally break through this long, collective dark night, the whole U.S. church, I believe, longs for a public ritual of lament for the thousands of children and teenagers abused by clergy, church personnel, coaches, scout leaders, teachers, and parents. The cries of anguish from Ramah to Boston, from Lafayette to Minneapolis, from Los Angeles to New York now partially smothered by the passage of time will continue to be raised until the Catholic imagination fashions some kind of liturgy of lament to heal and soothe the present pain.

In the meantime, the faithful daring to speak will do so from exile and from their deep pain. They want to "come home" to a church that has for too long treated them as less than full, adult members with gifts to be employed for the mission of the church. They link the abundance of wasted talent with the anguish of starving people who observe wasted food that could feed the multitudes. Like exiles throughout history, the faithful dwell in a strange place, geographically at home, but estranged from church authorities that fail to listen, fail to understand. Around kitchen tables rather than by the side of the rivers of Babylon, they tell their stories of faith to their children and grandchildren fearing even in the telling the loss of faith for the generations to come. Some have made peace with their estrangement, with their exile in place, and have given up all hope for a renewed church. They exist without community or sacraments, without hope sustained by the preaching of the gospel, and soon fail to understand their souls' true hunger. They get on with their lives as best they can. From time to time, they suspect they have never been missed.

Other exiles in place struggle as all exiles do simply to survive. They clearly are tired of surviving as Catholics and desire now to flourish and to see their children flourish. They have learned the lessons of exile: mature faith, patient endurance, sustaining memory. The hurt and anger of the prolonged estrangement of exile can be heard in the passion and pathos of their voices. But so, too, can their faith, their tenacity, their hope rooted in memory. Underneath the hurt and anger, moreover, they remain disciples, God's holy people.

From Whence the Voices Rise

As we have seen, faithful voices will emerge from virtual exile and from out of deep grief and lament. They will be voices that crack with emotion, with faith and hope and hurt. They also will be voices that resonate with strength and conviction, with confidence and resolve. The voices we hear will speak wisdom— and sometimes foolishness. They will heal—and sometimes wound. They will prompt us to cheer—and sometimes to cringe. But they will be the voices of God's people, priests and religious, married and single, educated and unlettered, young and old, of every stripe and color. They will be sisters and brothers united by a common baptism. And the Spirit will be upon them guiding them to see and embrace the truth they hear as well as to reject the folly that is spoken.

From the Vatican and chancery. Throughout his long reign, Pope John Paul II has dared to speak prophetically about economic justice and human dignity to the consumerist cultures of the world. He has defended the value of human life to the "cultures of death." The powerless, the poor, and the exploited of the world will continue to hear a firm and strong voice of hope and support from the bishop of Rome speaking to the power elites and calling for economic and social reform. And many bishops will continue to honor their office with prophetic cries for a more just social order based on the dignity of the individual and regard for the common good.

From the rectory. Growing numbers of priests and lay pastoral ministers will claim their integrity as preachers of the word without regard for their careers and the criticism of the establishment. As coworkers with their bishops, priests will speak to the social issues of their day—from hunger and homelessness to the dignity of gay and lesbian Catholics. They will speak candidly to their bishops from their personal and pastoral experience about the changes necessary if priests are to lead healthier, more mature adult lives. They will decry the forced fasting from Eucharist in many areas of the church. They will seek without faltering review of the church law requiring celibacy for diocesan priests of the Latin rite. They will speak to their married brother priests about how they might return to some form of ministry in the church. And they will speak to their parishioners of their desire to listen well and minister effectively.

Priests appear to be shedding their usual reticence to speak directly and candidly to their bishops. They know what their bishops want to hear and what they don't want to hear. Fear of displeasing their bishop, subtle and not so subtle careerism, Oedipal tensions imbedded in the priestly fraternity contribute to their wariness of speaking out. Both their training in submissiveness and the clerical culture itself reinforce a less than mature docility and a more than appropriate deference to episcopal authority.

This troubling reticence of the clergy was noted with concern a half century ago by the church historian John Tracy Ellis. Ellis, I suspect, understood what was at stake in the clergy's cowering before their ecclesiastical superiors—the compromising of their integrity. In theologian and poet Kilian McDonnell's poem "The

Monastic Cemetery," the theme of integrity surfaces as he and his brother monks bury one of their confreres. "No grand betrayals / we lacked the impudent will / we died of small treasons." Diocesan priests might well make a similar confession: "No grand betrayals / we lacked the moral courage / we died of small treasons." Clearly the majority of priests are not guilty of "grand betrayals,"—they have not abused their authority, they have not abused children, they have not appropriated parish or diocesan funds. But, nonetheless, a growing number understand their integrity is at stake if they maintain an unholy silence when their pastoral experience and personal convictions demand that they speak. They fear they are dying of small treasons. Playing their cards too close to their vest, they understand, is a form of cowardice, a series of small betrayals that nevertheless chips away at their integrity. More and more priests, with quiet courage and resolve, are choosing an authentic life that honors their soul's integrity over the soul-shrinking deaths of small treasons. Poet Audre Lorde's testimony to daring speech upon hearing of her life threatening cancer diagnosis resonates with their own quest for integrity:

> In becoming forcibly and essentially aware of my mortality, and of what I wished and wanted for my life, however short it might be, priorities and omissions became strongly etched in a merciless light, and what I most regretted were my silences. Of what had I *ever* been afraid? To question or to speak as I believed could have meant pain, or death. But we all hurt in so many different ways, all the time, and pain will either change or end. Death, on the other hand, is the final silence. And that might be coming quickly, now, without regard for whether I had ever spoken what needed to be said, or had only betrayed myself into small silences, while I planned someday to speak, or waited for someone else's words. And I began to recognize a source of power within myself that comes from the knowledge that while it is most desirable not to be afraid, learning to put fear into perspective gave me great strength ("The Transformation of Silence into Language and Action," in *Sister Outsider*, The Crossing Press, 1984).

Emerging signs in the present church crisis point to a growing conviction that it is the *laity's moment*. How the laity respond to the scandals and to the undeniable need for church reform will be critical, even though the ecclesial deck is stacked against them. The institutional and canonical cards, after all, are in the hands of the Vatican curia. If the priests of western Europe and North America find their voice and courage, a holy alliance will be forged with the laity that will in turn shape the future of the church in the northern hemisphere.

From the monastery and convent. Vowed religious will continue to witness radical fidelity to the gospel and model democratic forms of church governance. They will remind laity and clergy of the gospel call to simplicity of life, of the dangers of power, of humility's liberation. Contemplative religious will employ the "sounds of silence" to remind church and society of the need for solitude and reflection. Apostolic religious will bear witness to the common vocation to serve and care for the least among us.

Without question, monastic voices have been among the most powerful prophetic voices both in church and society. And these voices have disturbed and troubled both church and society. Why else forbid Thomas Merton at the height of the Cold War from publishing on issues relating to war and peace? A listing of monks, friars, and other vowed religious who were silenced by their superiors, often so ordered by church authorities, is long indeed. Thinkers and writers such as Marie-Dominique Chenu, Yves Congar, Teilhard de Chardin, John Courtney Murray, Hans Küng, Charles Curran, and Jacques Dupuis, each representing hundreds of other scholars so silenced, have dared "to speak their truth in love" (St. Catherine of Siena).

These men and women have dared to speak unwelcome words, to name difficult truths, to ask troubling questions. They have pointed to and protested policies and systems held sacred by the hierarchy that nonetheless inhibit the vitality and mission of the church. Paternalism, sexism, and clericalism have each felt the heat of their protest. "Obviously, the monastic life is nothing," wrote Thomas Merton, "if it does not open a man wide to the Holy Spirit. In actual fact, the head-in-the-ground type of monk is usually in practice the most damnable fascist you ever saw" (from a letter to Daniel Berrigan in *The Hidden Ground of Love: The Letters of Thomas Merton on Religious Experience and Social Concerns*).

Timothy Radcliffe, the previous Master of the Dominicans, has dared to speak with the most prophetic of the world's monks and friars. In his reflection on Vatican II's *Gaudium et Spes,* Radcliffe writes, "Dialogue is fruitful when it is the struggle to learn from each other. The medieval *disputatio* practiced by St. Thomas was based on the assumption that one's opponent is always, in some sense, right. It is easy to identify another person's errors. Do we have the courage to hear what they may teach us? . . . This demands of us vulnerability" *(Sing a New Song: The Christian Vocation).*

What would happen if church authorities took Radcliffe's words to heart? What would happen if the faithful took Radcliffe's words to heart? The present polarization would be softened and the current cultural wars pitting conservatives and progressives against each other might find grounds for a truce. Differing parties would look for that which was right in their opponents' position. The tone and tenor of church dialogue would change dramatically. Laity, vowed religious, clergy, and prelates would listen with new ears. They would catch, I believe, whisperings of the Spirit.

Monks, nuns, and friars, like all who take the gospel seriously, open themselves wide to the Holy Spirit. It should not surprise us to find in their writing seeds of hope, wisdom, and reform.

From faithful writers and speakers. During the four decades since my ordination as a priest, I have come to know a few men and women who have dared to speak and write from the wellsprings of their faith in God and their love of the church. Their courage in the face of secret inquiries into the orthodoxy of their work has inspired me to be half as courageous. A number of these writers have undergone formal investigations by various Vatican congregations. The weight of the ordeal was evident in eyes that reflected fatigue from countless hours responding to written questions of clarification. There was a palpable sadness behind their brave smiles—a sadness welling up from official concern about their fidelity to the gospel they had served throughout their adult lives. Some of their cases have become public. Others remain known only to trusted friends.

A number of Catholic journals have dared to speak the truth—*America, Commonweal, U.S. Catholic, The Tablet,* and, in particular, the *National Catholic Reporter.* Let me mention but two examples of the *NCR's* courage. The *NCR's* publisher, editor, and staff suffered an avalanche of criticism in the early 1980s for breaking the clergy sexual abuse crisis and for their coverage of the sexual abuse of religious women by priests in Africa and elsewhere in the 1990s. The *NCR* was accused of church-bashing when it dared to report what it knew to be true—suffering significant personal, spiritual, and financial retribution. These publishers and editors dared to speak the truth because their own integrity demanded it, their faith insisted upon it.

Among the many Catholics writing and speaking from a committed, mature faith perspective about the clergy abuse scandals, Margaret O'Brien Steinfels, former editor of *Commonweal* and the University of Notre Dame's Scott Appleby were invited, along with victim survivors Craig Martin and David Clohessy, and psychologist Mary Gail Frawley-O'Dea, to speak to the U.S. bishops at their watershed meeting in Dallas in June 2002.

For the previous five months the bishops had endured the sting of angry and harsh public criticism for their mishandling of the scandal. The criticism came from victims, their parents, and their attorneys, from the print media, from demonstrators outside their chanceries and cathedrals, from television and radio commentators. At their Dallas meeting, however, they heard directly what they seldom heard before as bishops: strong, intelligent, articulate, heartfelt words of rebuke and challenge. Many listened with what Walter Brueggemann has described as "royal consciousness," an attitude of heart and mind out of touch with the needs and concerns of the people. We might think of it as "prelatial consciousness," the limited vision and courtly compassion of prelates who have lost touch with their people—bishops who have taken too seriously their episcopal status. These bishops seemed to think of themselves as "not like the rest of men." Some among them surely said under their breath, "How dare they!" "Do they know to whom they are speaking?" As a body of ecclesiastics long accustomed to signs of deference and respect, some appeared untouched by the grace of "self-doubt."

The real problem, Scott Appleby insisted, was deeper than the sexual abuse of children and minors by Catholic clergy. The very system of the church, its clerical way of doing things as a privileged society within society at large was at the heart of the problem. In his words:

> Whether the Catholic Church as currently governed and managed can proclaim the Gospel effectively in this milieu is an open question. I remind you that a remarkable, and to my mind encouraging, development in response to the danger we now face is that Catholics on the right and the left, and in the "deep middle" all are in basic agreement as to the causes of this scandal: a betrayal of fidelity enabled by the arrogance that comes with unchecked power. I do not exaggerate by saying that the future of the church in this country depends upon your sharing authority with the laity (www.usccb.org/bishops/appleby.htm).

The heart of Margaret O'Brien Steinfels' address to the bishops underscored the impotence the laity feel in the wake of the scandal:

> [W]hatever the causes of the scandal, the fact is that the dam has broken. A reservoir of trust among Catholics has run dry. This scandal has brought home to lay people how essentially powerless they are to affect its outcome—and virtually anything else to do with the church. When we ask, "What can I do?" what lay person isn't brought up short in realizing, forty years after Vatican II with

its promise of consultation and collaboration, that our only serious leverage is money? That in itself is a scandal.

Emphasizing the link between trust and truth, Steinfels continued:

When there is no genuine effort to build accountability and transparency into diocesan and parish governance; when we hear those rote phrases about the church not being a democracy, as if it were a system only of majority vote, and not also of checks and balances and of consultation; when we are unilaterally admonished against discussing some topics; when we know that so many bishops and priests cannot or will not say publicly what they really think, especially now when people long to hear an honest word of explanation, when the Vatican appears to place hopes for priestly vocations in the strict liturgical separation of the ordained and the lay, what conclusions can be drawn except that you don't trust us? (www.usccb.org/bishops/steinfels.htm).

Never before in the history of the U.S. church had the laity dared to speak so honestly and so forthrightly to their assembled episcopal pastors. Nor were the voices of Appleby and Steinfels the only voices the bishops heard. Victim/survivors Martin and Clohessy spoke of abuse and betrayal from wells of deep pain and crushing sadness.

Describing the bishops' observable response to Martin's presentation, David Gibson writes, "This was Craig Martin's personal psalmody, a cry of utter isolation and rejection. But for all of the emotion on the dais, it was hard to gauge the bishops' reaction. Some may have been moved. Most sat quietly, or fidgeted, or looked down at the papers in front of them" *(The Coming Catholic Church)*.

Taking the measure of the bishops' response to David Clohessy's address, Gibson noted:

The impact of Clohessy's words was also unclear. Although Bishop Wilton Gregory (president of the U.S. Conference of Catholic Bishops) had received a standing ovation after his opening address and Appleby and Steinfels had been greeted with polite applause, the victims received a more constrained response, a courtesy carefully measured out.

How do we explain such "controlled compassion"? Before all else, bishops are pastors. Yet, according to Gibson's account, there was no clear pastoral response to the wounds and anguish evident in the voices of Martin and Clohessy.

Scott Appleby, Margaret O'Brien Steinfels, Mary Gail Frawley-O'Dea, Craig Martin, and David Clohessy dared to speak to the guardians of faith from their own deep faith and from their love for the church. Heard or not, they earned the respect and gratitude of countless Catholics for the witness of their courage and faith. Drawing upon lifetimes of fidelity to the gospel and church, they dared to confront and challenge their episcopal brothers.

Bishop Wilton Gregory and Archbishop Harry Flynn who invited the "outside" speakers to the Dallas meeting dared to do something most unusual and yet necessary. I suspect they endured criticism from some quarters of the gathered bishops. I hope they also heard words of affirmation and gratitude.

From the university. The university's role in society reaches beyond the education and formation of its students. Catholic universities and colleges embrace this vision with particular fervor and their mission statements regularly point to the institution's commitment to provide both intellectual and moral leadership and an appropriate forum to address issues affecting the common good. A number of Catholic universities have made major contributions in recent years to furthering the public's understanding of the nature and causes of the abuse scandal as well as to address the broader ecclesial and theological issues that spawned the present crisis. These institutions have sponsored conferences and lecture series that have critically assessed the historical, theological, canonical, structural, and pastoral dimensions of arguably the most critical moment in the history of the U.S. Catholic church.

President William Leahy, S.J., of Boston College, for example, inaugurated "The Church in the 21st Century Initiative," a comprehensive two-year program addressing the church's crisis with a candor and forthrightness not often seen in church circles. The initiative's objective is to explore three broad topics directly related to the crisis: the roles of laity, priests, and bishops in the church; a contemporary understanding of sexuality in light of Catholic beliefs; and the challenges Catholics face in living, deepening, and handing on the faith to future generations. To maximize the audience for "The Church in the 21st Century Initiative," the university is publishing *C21 Resources*, a six-issue report that reprints "articles and presentations on the current crisis in the church and the path to renewal."

Another important initiative was undertaken by the leadership of St. Thomas More Chapel, the Catholic Center at Yale University. The chapel's board of trustees authorized the chaplain, Robert Beloin, to appoint a committee to organize a conference titled, "Governance, Accountability, and the Future of the Church," which was held at the chapel and the Yale Law School on March 28–30, 2003. The conferences' presentations were published under the editorship of Francis Oakley and Bruce Russett in *Governance, Accountability, and the Future of the Catholic Church* (Continuum, 2004).

The conferences and publications sponsored by Boston College and the St. Thomas More Chapel at Yale are notable for their depth and comprehensive treatment of the church's unprecedented crisis. Numerous other Catholic colleges and universities, from coast to coast, sponsored and continue to sponsor conferences and lectures addressing the dark night engulfing today's church. They bear witness to a faith tradition that dares to speak the truth in love.

The courage for faith-filled speech continues to emerge from laity, vowed religious, priests, and bishops. As they dare to speak they shape a communion of truth seekers that is proving, I believe, to be a lifeline of hope for all who treasure the gospel and the communion of disciples we call church. Their voices, as we shall see in chapter 8, are converging into a chorus of voices—voices welling up from an invincible hope calling for a renewed social order and a renewed church. "[Y]ou will," in the words of Second Isaiah, "rebuild the ancient ruins; you will raise up the age-old foundations; and you will be called the repairer of the breach, the restorer of the streets in which to dwell" (see Isa 58:12).

CHAPTER FIVE

THE LIBERATION
OF THE LAITY

There is no distinction between "laypeople" and "clerics" in the vocabulary of the New Testament.

—Yves Congar

In the New Testament, the priest is presented as an ideal layman. But almost immediately there begins his increasingly radical separation from lay people; and not only separation, but opposition to lay people, contrast to them.

—Alexander Schmemann

The exercise of authority without accountability is not servant-leadership: it is tyranny.

—Report of the National Review Board

IN CHAPTER ONE I proposed that the present crisis is pregnant with the grace of the Spirit and that the path of deliverance for the church is likely to be forged by the broadest segment of the people of God, the laity. It is, as you may recall, the *laity's moment*—a moment of redemptive honesty where the grace of initiative and leadership rests primarily, though not exclusively, with the baptized disciples of Jesus.

This is not to minimize or to downplay the importance and significance of the ordained leaders of the church. It is, however, to underscore the vital and necessary role of the laity in the affairs of the church—a role that has finally been confirmed by the Second

Vatican Council. In spite of the council's affirmation of the active role of the laity in the life and mission of the church, we have seen in recent decades a major re-entrenchment by powerful curial and episcopal archconservatives. Clasping tightly to a pre-conciliar understanding of the church, they continue to see the church as a perfect society made up of two unequal segments: the superior level of episcopal pastors and the inferior segment of the docile flock, the laity, whose sole responsibility is to follow the dictates of the hierarchy as obedient sheep.

The disquieting movement back to pre-conciliar attitudes and ideologies is undergirded and supported by entrenched, powerful Vatican officials—at least for the time being. But, as we have seen, the sexual abuse scandal and especially the leadership scandal that ensued have nudged the laity out of their passivity and submissiveness into an awakened awareness of their dignity and proper role as full, adult members of the church. Never again will they tolerate being treated as naïve children who must be protected from scandal at all costs. Never again, at least in countries and cultures where Catholics are well educated, will the deferential subservience of past generations be the dominant attitude of the faithful. Vatican II, World War II, and the present crisis have finally and irrevocably subverted the "pray, pay, and obey" mentality of bygone days. Vatican II's Constitution on the Church, Constitution on the Church in the Modern World, and its Decree on the Laity built upon and ratified the theologies of the laity developed in the nineteenth century by John Henry Newman and in the 1930s by Dominicans Dominique Marie Chenu and Yves Congar and Jesuits Henri de Lubac and Jean Danielou.

The laity were emancipated. For U.S. veterans, World War II led to the G.I. Bill and the opportunity for blue collar Catholics to obtain college educations previously beyond their financial means.

The laity were well educated. Many of the laity now held graduate degrees in religious education, pastoral ministry, theology, and Scripture. Liberated and educated, they discovered they could think and reason and reflect—the hallmarks of adulthood.

Preaching to highly educated Catholics presented a different challenge to pastors preparing their Sunday homilies. Not infrequently,
the people in the pews knew more theology and Scripture than
the priest in the pulpit. And in working class parishes, the life experiences of the people in the pews were often more real, more
immediate, than the preachers.

Catholic laity were coming of age. The church in North America, we came to see, would never be the same. Catholics now expected compelling rationales for the moral teachings of the church
and for its disciplines and practices, for its structures and systems
of governance. Pastors could no longer fall back on authoritarian
assertions that proved sufficient in past generations to elicit compliance and submission from the laity. This signaled not a lessening
of faith, but a more mature faith on the part of the laity.

For many bishops and priests, it signaled a daunting new era of
pastoral leadership and church governance. Many of the old securities were gone. The unearned deference and respect of generations
past were gone. The comforts and privileges of clerical culture were
being discussed with derision. Priests, especially, found themselves
working harder than ever with fewer of the supports and perks that
had long made the demands of parish ministry and the discipline of
celibacy somewhat lighter. While their office was respected, they
now had to personally earn the respect of their parishioners. And
while their parishioners didn't demand or even expect perfection,
they did expect them to be *real*—to be authentic human beings able
to understand their struggles and sorrows. The laity, most priests
understood, wanted leadership, not domination.

While the post-Vatican II church proved more disquieting for
a good number of priests, bishops, and pastoral ministers, the laity
participated in parish life with a new appreciation of their dignity
and a renewed identity as full and equal members of the church.
The impact of the laity's more active role in parish life is telling—
the Catholic church in America is arguably one of the most vital
and vibrant churches in the world. In spite of a dramatic drop in
the number of Catholics attending Mass each Sunday (down from

approximately 70 percent in the 1960s to less than 30 percent in the first years of the new millennium) parish life, social outreach, and personal faith commitment are strong in many of the more than nineteen thousand U.S. parishes.

When compared to the practice of the faith and parish life in traditionally Catholic European countries—France, Spain, Belgium, and Italy—it appears quite vibrant indeed. Moreover, the very vitality and maturity found in the faith lives of U.S. Catholics is matched by the intellectual and spiritual maturation of the faithful. Neuralgic church issues that many would have suffered silently just decades ago are now raised at meetings of the parish pastoral council and the diocesan pastoral council. Without question, many parishes remain under the firm thumb of authoritarian pastors. Yet, a critical mass has been reached of faithful, articulate, and intelligent laity who are profoundly changing the face of American church life. Still, the struggle for liberation continues.

You Are the Church—but . . .

For decades now, Catholics have heard they are the church. But for the most part they haven't experienced the full reality of such declarations. Australian Bishop John Heaps recounts an exchange between Catholic laity and a Catholic bishop. The issue of priests who had married and who were thereby barred from any form of liturgical ministry was raised. "Where is the compassion of the church?" the bishop was asked. He answered that the church showed great compassion in its care of the sick, the poor, and the homeless. It was a response the laity had heard time and time again. They are the church when it comes to visiting the sick, feeding the hungry, and sheltering the homeless. They are the church when it comes to supporting the parish and diocese, when it comes to pledges for Catholic Charities and other ministries for the needy. But when it comes to a meaningful voice in shaping decisions that touch directly upon their lives or in the making of rules or in the exercising of church governance, they remain outsiders.

Over the years, especially during my assignment as vicar for clergy and religious, I came to know firsthand the struggles of priests who clearly possessed the charism of ordained leadership but also felt an equally compelling call to marriage. Fidelity to their own integrity and respect for the church led most of these men to apply for laicization—the Vatican's administrative action that returned them to the lay state and permitted them, often after a civil marriage had taken place, to be married "in the church." The decree of laicization was accompanied by a number of painful restrictions. No longer could the laicized priest even proclaim the Scriptures at Eucharist; nor could he be a eucharistic minister or catechist or religious educator. Moreover, he was forbidden to teach theology in Catholic schools and colleges. The rationale for these prohibitions appears to be the Vatican's fear that the laity would be confused if a married priest ministered as a lector or distributed the Eucharist. Many think they are punitive—blocking the laicized priest from liturgical roles and ministries the laity may exercise.

Adult, Vatican II Catholics remain largely unaware of these prohibitions. How might they react to such restrictions? Probably with the following assertions: "Ask us whether or not we would be confused or scandalized." "Don't assume you know what scandalizes us." "Ask us whether or not we would welcome married men as our pastors." "Ask us about more meaningful ministries for women." As adults, the laity bristle when they are told what will confuse them or scandalize them. They feel patronized when they are told what is good for them—when they are told the institutional church and the bishops know best. They have heard a good deal about consultation and collaboration and cooperation. They have heard about the responsibilities and obligations of the laity—that Vatican II "sought to give the laity an active life in the church and in the development of doctrine" in the words of Cardinal Avery Dulles (A People Adrift, 260). This they know. Yet they have seen their initiatives met with suspicion, their calls for structural reform ignored, their abused children kept at distance. They are the church, but . . . .

Lay Leadership on Chancery Staffs

Catholic laity in general and lay church leaders in particular sense an unholy tension pulling at the heartstrings of their faith. Those who are well read know Vatican II's major themes of liberation. They know they are equal members with their ordained brothers in the universal family of the church. They know that the Spirit of God roams the corridors of their souls as it roams the halls of the curia. They know their gifts are important, indeed critical, to the mission of the church. This they know. They know, too, that in some dioceses, forward looking bishops have named lay men and women as well as religious to the post of chancellor and other key positions such as vicar for education or parish life. While bishops appointing lay men and women to key diocesan positions may be in the minority, they are still signs of the laity's liberation.

Even when laity and vowed religious hold one or more of the relatively few major diocesan staff positions awarded to the non-ordained, they often feel as if they are junior members in the eyes of their clerical colleagues. They suspect, often when it isn't the case at all, that they have been brought inside as tokens, much like the African American appointed in decades past to a relatively high governmental post to assuage the heated calls for racial inclusivity. When it comes to specific issues of church governance, these lay and vowed religious often remain outsiders. And when some appear to have affected a breakthrough into the "official family" (as one diocesan bureaucrat put it), they not infrequently become as clerical as their ordained confreres. It is as if they have been welcomed into the club and the initiation fee is their repudiation of their lay status. To the degree that this happens, they are already compromised. They begin to experience the minor pain, the existential guilt—almost unnoticed—that follows upon the loss of their integrity.

Not long ago I spoke with a highly placed lay diocesan official who had worked for his diocese for more than twenty years.

He had the insight and courage to admit that he feared from time to time that he was being co-opted by the system—that he was becoming "clerical." I wanted to tell him not to worry. The very fact that he sensed the danger was his deliverance. A number of his lay colleagues, it must be noted, were not as astute. They had become, they thought, insiders. And their loyalty now was to the institutional church rather than to the gospel and to the faithful they served. Often enough a certain inner glow wells up in the relatively few lay people brought into important and sometimes prominent positions in a diocesan curia. They had, by all appearances, cracked the glass ceiling. But the clerical club ultimately belongs to the ordained, an elite enclosed caste whose defining characteristics include celibacy and maleness. Sooner or later most core-staff laity come to understand they will always be outsiders to the members of the caste. Their lay status in the clerical world of chancery politics was something they could never completely shed. The important cards were still held by the "collars."

This may be the case on the core staffs of many large U.S. dioceses. Away from the power-centers, however, the situation is significantly different. In Catholic schools, hospitals, social service agencies, and a growing number of parishes, leadership in recent decades has moved from the clergy and vowed religious to lay women and men. In these church institutions lay leadership is flourishing, and it is the cleric who may feel like the outsider. The competence and commitment of lay leaders in so many areas of church life as well as in secular life continue the liberation of the laity inspired by the council.

Following the renewal and reform of Vatican II, the realization has taken hold that the church will never be the same again. Following the scandalous decisions made by numerous bishops responding to the clergy sexual abuse scandals, this realization is now firmly grounded in the minds and hearts of the lay faithful— the church will never be the same again. That being the case, what might a renewed and reformed church look like?

In Search of an Accountable Church

Both the title of this chapter and the "search for an account-able church" were taken from Paul Lakeland's important 2003 book, *The Liberation of the Laity: In Search of an Accountable Church*. Here Lakeland gives us nothing less than a blueprint for the future of the church—and the major role the laity will play in this church. Most readers, I believe, would be wise to accept the author's suggestion to begin not at the beginning, that is chapter one, but rather to enter this rich volume at part II, "Where We Go from Here." Part I, however, is not to be missed. Lakeland lays out here critical historical and theological dimensions that undergird the constructive thrust of part II. How we got to this present moment of crisis, why it is so paralyzing to some and so liberating to others, and how we might move into the future are laid out in this compelling book. What follows in this chapter is largely a commentary on the second part of Lakeland's *The Liberation of the Laity*.

We ask here the implicit question nestled within the previous chapters of this book as well as in the title of Lakeland's book: from what are the laity in need of liberation? Simply and starkly put—they are in need of liberation from structural oppression. An oppression, moreover, of which many of the laity remain unaware and an oppression to which some, as we shall see, are complicitous. Surely most bishops and other church officials think of themselves as pastors, teachers, and administrators rather than oppressors. What they do, unpopular as it often is, they do for the good of the church. To their minds, if they are controlling, inflexible, and enforcers of church teaching it is because this is their responsibility.

Bishops and other church officials, however, sustain the laity's oppression when they sustain church structures—imperial, monarchical, and feudal—that keep the laity in subservient roles. Today's educated laity are quite capable of distinguishing between revealed church teaching and historically conditioned structures and systems of governance that no longer serve the wellbeing of the faithful nor the church's mission. No doubt many of the laity continue to work through their "adolescent" identity crisis, but they do so fully aware that their integrity is on the line. As they call for accountability from bishops and church authorities they are holding each other accountable as adult members of the church.

Identity. I began an earlier book, *The Changing Face of the Priesthood,* with a chapter titled "Discovering an Identity." It remains a fundamental issue for priests as they come to understand—both historically and theologically—their place and role in the life and mission of the post-conciliar church. So central is the issue of identity that if we get it right many of the more neuralgic issues challenging the church begin to dissolve or at least come into proper focus where they can be effectively addressed. And so it is with the laity. One of the most significant contributions of the council, we have seen, is the assertion that all the baptized are full and equal members of the church. ". . . [T]here is in Christ and the Church no inequality on the basis of race or nationality, social condition or sex, because 'there is neither Jew nor Greek; there is neither slave nor freeman; there is neither male nor female. For you are all one in Christ Jesus'" (Constitution on the Church, Part IV).

Yet the very identity of the laity as understood by Pius X, who envisioned the church as an unequal society made up of active shepherds (bishops and priests) and a passive flock, continues to be embraced as normative in reactionary circles of the church well into the twenty-first century. Since the council, it is understood that all baptized are full and equal members of the church with obviously different ministries and responsibilities. The passive role attributed to the laity in centuries past has been rejected. They now stand in the assembly of believers as adult members of a holy communion—the body of Christ—sustained and guided by the presence of God's Spirit dwelling in their midst. With bishops and vowed religious, with theologians and catechists, with preachers and pastors, with curial officials and diocesan authorities, they stand in the assembly and declare, "*Adsum:* I am present." With the entire church, with their brothers and sisters in Christ, they claim no other identity than *disciple of Jesus the Christ*. So much falls into place when the believer's primary identity is that of disciple. So much is obfuscated when we exaggerate the lay/clergy distinction. For the greater part of the church's history, we have defined the laity as non-clergy rather than reflecting on the role of the ordained as first and fundamentally members of the faithful—as disciples—called by the Spirit and the community to essential roles of leadership in the liturgical and pastoral life of the church. Lakeland underscores the insight of Yves Congar and Edward Schillebeeckx that "it is the clergy relative to the laity, not the laity to the clergy, that is in need of explanation."

When the celibate, all-male clergy lost sight of their primary identity as disciples and over-identified with their ministerial priest-hood, a caste system evolved that psychologically isolated them from the non-ordained and insulated them from the every-day struggles of most believers. A culture of control, secrecy, and supe-riority emerged. Only the authentically humble escaped the arro-gance and elitism of this clerical culture. When the laity were led to suppress their primary identity as adult disciples of the Christ and full and equal members of the church, they became passive recipients of the ministrations of the clergy. Their ecclesial world shrunk to concern for the salvation of their souls.

Many of the laity welcomed this passive, receptive mode of being a Catholic Christian. There was a certain clarity and simplic-ity to it. Keep the commandments, believe without question or re-flection what the church teaches, and support the financial needs of the parish and diocese—and all would be well. In the process, however, many became complicit in their own structural oppres-sion. The daily, existential demands of living one's life in light of the gospel could be quieted by adapting an attitude of passive, noncritical receptivity to church authorities. Most of the laity, even the vast majority of the laity, expected little or no account-ability from church leaders. Nor was transparency into the gov-ernance and financial spheres of the church expected. This all began to change, we have seen, in the decades leading up to Vatican II, in the council itself, and in the jarring, tragic, wake-up call the laity received in the wake of the clergy sexual abuse scandal. The laity now understand that it is indeed their moment. If they are to maintain their integrity, silence is no longer an option.

Integrity. While many Catholics remain more or less satisfied with a passive and less than fully adult role in the church, an ever-growing number of the baptized are not. Both Vatican II and World War II's G.I. Bill, as we have seen, have lifted up the laity to see beyond their culture of adolescent passivity to their rightful place as adult members of the church. They, too, sense that they are in danger of "dying of small treasons." Keeping silent, they now understand, may well be a small treason. Remaining passive in the face of the abuse crisis may well be a small treason. And small treasons, like major treasons, corrode one's integrity. Treasons and betrayals, large or small, inevitably lead to a complicitous complacency. Without necessarily recognizing it, individuals become compromised. Having heard the wake-up call, it is no longer relatively easy for the laity (and clergy), in the words of Christopher Bollas in his *Being a Character,* "to be innocent of a troubling recognition": the church is in need of renewal and structural reform.

The laity now recognize more clearly than they have for centuries the need for an accountable church—a fundamental step toward renewal and reform. Their own integrity as the people of God demands that they drink from the waters of courage and insist on nothing less than the accountability and transparency that is their due as full members of the body of Christ. Their own integrity—their conscience—dares them to question, dares them to speak. They sense in the marrow of their bones that should they remain silent not only will the church be poorer for it, their own souls will suffer a crisis of integrity.

Daring to question, daring to speak—especially to power—implies a certain risk. Risk taking, most would agree, is inherent to an authentic life well lived. It is also inherent to a life of integrity. Individuals who never take risks do indeed die of small treasons.

And they risk the great treason of leading an inauthentic life: a life of "quiet desperation." Discipleship requires the fundamental risk of faith—to throw in one's lot with the people of God. And faith in God requires that the disciple risks speaking her truth in love in the power of the Spirit and in the name of Jesus. Some will surely misunderstand. Others will surely criticize. Still others will condemn. But like the prophets, disciples cannot but dare to speak.

Accountability. It is a new day for the laity. The abuse scandal has proved to be the tipping point taking them over and beyond a distant horizon. Now they see more clearly than ever their adult identity as the Spirit-sustained people of God. Standing now in the liberating rays of a morning light, the laity vow never again to submit unthinkingly to authoritarian control. They are willing to forgo the former securities afforded them by their passive role in the church and to stand tall in the presence of their fellow disciples. Silence, they now understand, is no longer an option. As they dare to speak it becomes clear that their first responsibility is to call each other as laity to accountability. Painful questions surface as they do so. Has their naivete been as innocent as it might seem? Have they unwittingly been complicitous in their own oppression? Have they more or less unconsciously ignored responsibilities inherent to adult discipleship?

Ecclesial adulthood, they discover, is far more demanding than ecclesial adolescence. As the laity demand accountability and transparency from church leaders and officials, they must reflect seriously on their own accountability to each other, to their bishops and pastors, and above all, on their accountability to the gospel. Pastors and parochial ministers likewise must take the measure of their accountability to one another, to their parishioners as well as to their ecclesial superiors.

Accountable themselves to the church, the laity now expect nothing less than accountability from their bishops—an accountability the U.S. bishops themselves have promised. Yet, as we shall see below, it is an accountability that is slow in coming.

The National Review Board Report

On February 27, 2004, the National Review Board, established to examine the nature and causes of the clergy sexual abuse scandal, issued its report to widespread news coverage. It was by all accounts a significant moment in the history of the U.S. Catholic church. From the perspective of the U.S. Conference of Catholic Bishops, which appointed the board, the report itself was a demonstration of the bishops' promise to accountability. From the perspective of the laity, it was their symbolic *independence day*—their liberation day—even though their liberation is still very much in process. What they knew in their hearts about the nonfeasance and malfeasance of many bishops was confirmed in the board's candid and comprehensive report: the historically conditioned clerical structures of church governance and accountability were not working and had subjected thousands of children to the agonies of sexual abuse at the hands of clergy. If there was any doubt about the role and responsibility of bishops in the scandal, it ended with the release and publication of the review board's report. Since February of 2004, it will be difficult, though clearly not impossible, for bishops to act paternalistically and without accountability in the exercise of episcopal authority.

The following excerpts of the review board's report and statements by the board's research committee each reflect and further the liberation of the laity:

- "The exercise of authority without accountability is not servant leadership; it is tyranny."—National Review Board
- "An individual bishop is virtually an absolute power; they are virtually unaccountable . . . I am by no means confident that they will make the basic changes that have to be made in governance. And at the end of the day if they don't, I think there are going to be . . . other problems."—Robert Bennett (Chair of the board's research committee, *National Catholic Reporter*, March 12, 2004)

- "I think we were all surprised at the level of secrecy in the hierarchy. I think we now understand one meaning of the First Estate. The ability to control minds on the basis of God is incredible. There are no women in this country (referring to the world of the hierarchy). . . . The bishops are an odd group of people, very insular."—Pamela Hayes (review board member, *NCR*, March 12, 2004)

- "These dioceses are separate fiefdoms. It's an almost medieval organization we're dealing with. Each bishop runs his own fiefdom. There is very little communication between those bishops and indeed, very little communication between bishops and the Vatican. The basic culture that developed is, 'We take care of our own, we really don't want to open ourselves up to being questioned by others.' The key here is going to be whether there is greater participation by the laity. I am not sure that there's enough pressure internally to really produce the changes that are necessary. I say that because in some of the interviews with the hierarchy there was clearly the sense that they were anxious to get this whole thing behind them—back to business as usual."—Leon Panetta (review board member, *NCR*, March 12, 2004)

- "There can be no doubt that while it is a gift for some, celibacy is a terrible burden for others, resulting in loneliness, alcohol and drug abuse, and improper sexual conduct . . . that demands further study."—National Review Board.

At a press conference immediately following the release of the National Review Board's Report, Bishop Wilton Gregory, president of the U.S. Conference of Catholic Bishops, declared: "The terrible history recorded here today is history." Gregory made explicit what Catholic laity had suspected for some time. The bishops believe they have been accountable to the faithful because they have apologized for their mistakes and for the abuse of children by their clergy, because they have established a national zero-tolerance policy for dealing with reports of clergy sexual abuse, because they have tried to settle fairly financial claims of victims, because a number of them have met personally with victims as the chief pastors of their dioceses, because they have established a national office for the protection of children and young people, and because they established the National Review Board and sponsored the John Jay College of Criminal Justice's empirical study measuring the scope and financial cost of the scandal.

For all of these initiatives the bishops clearly are to be commended. Their efforts, especially their commissioning of the John Jay study and the National Review Board's report, have provided an important service to both the church and the larger community by pointing to the widespread occurrence of sexual abuse of minors in society itself.

It appears, however, that many bishops want desperately what Bishop Gregory implied, to get the scandal behind them and get back to the way things were before the abuse scandals erupted. What many bishops don't realize is that a liberated laity won't let them. Following the leadership of victim/survivor groups, the laity appear not at all satisfied with the accountability thus far evidenced by the bishops. While bishops are quite ready to hold their priests to a problematic zero-tolerance policy, they have not been ready to hold brother bishops accountable for their cover-ups and reassigning of abuser priests. True accountability requires this.

"We are a sinful church. We are naked. Our anger, our pain, our anguish, our shame and our vulnerability are clear to the whole world. . . . I'm prepared to take the responsibility, and that's something I have to live with," said Archbishop Alphonsus Penney of Newfoundland, Canada, as he resigned his post following a highly critical report by a committee he had appointed to assess his handling of sexual abuse cases in his archdiocese (*NCR*, March 12, 2004) . U.S. Catholics are looking for similar examples of accountability and responsibility from their bishops. An educated, liberated laity knows the scandal and the crisis it spawned will not be over until meaningful structural reform and renewal are achieved. Such structural reform and renewal will fail if the liberated laity are not meaningful players in the process.

The clergy sexual abuse scandal, perhaps more than any other impetus, even Vatican II, has liberated the U.S. Catholic faithful. What the classic texts of the council failed to do—to communicate to the everyday Catholic layperson in language that he or she could readily understand—was accomplished by the aftermath of the abuse scandal. Anger, better outrage, brought the silent multitude of lay disciples of Jesus to say, "Enough. This is our church, too. And we want to save it for our children and grandchildren." The U.S. church will never be the same.

CHAPTER SIX

VOICE OF THE FAITHFUL

. . . [T]he job of priests with respect to lay people is not to make them the *longa manus* of the clergy, telling them what they've got to do; but to make them believing men and women, adult Christians, leaving them to meet and fulfill the concrete demands of their Christianity on their own responsibility and in accordance with their own consciences.

—Yves Congar

We deplore, and hold ourselves morally bound, to protest and resist, in church and society, all actions, customs, laws, and structures that treat women or men as less than fully human. We pledge ourselves to carry forth the heritage of biblical justice which mandates that all persons share in right relationships with each other, with the cosmos, and with the Creator.

—The Madeleva Manifesto

Great spirits have always encountered violent opposition from mediocre minds.

—Albert Einstein

SPEAKING ONE'S TRUTH IN LOVE, we have seen in previous chapters, is no simple matter. In the present restorationist climate and culture, one *dares* to speak. Nevertheless, many faithful Catholics now feel compelled to speak if not directly to church authorities then through membership in various renewal organizations. They are discovering on an existential level what it means to be adult members of the church. Although most appear to be middle aged and beyond, they are sensing the same exhilarating energy and freedom that younger adults feel when making the decisions that define them as adults and that mark definitively their passage from adolescence. Breaking through deeply entrenched church systems that determined their largely passive role for centuries demanded a certain braveness of heart. Having mustered the courage for the first step, they find successive steps easier. Sometimes all that is said can be distilled to *Adsum,* "I am here, I am present as a full, equal, adult member of the church—and I expect to be treated as such by church authorities."

What percentage of the faithful—and the faithful includes *all* disciples: laity, vowed religious, and clergy—are taking this symbolic step is, of course, difficult to determine. My suspicion is that we are much closer than we may think to the tipping point or critical mass required to bring about meaningful structural renewal and reform. What is certain is that large numbers of the people of God are finding their voice. No longer intimidated by episcopal warnings and prohibitions barring them from meeting on church property, they continue to assert their right to assemble as faithful members of the church. Bishops and other church officials are discovering that these organizations are not going away. It is simply no longer possible to stifle their calls for accountability, transparency, and for appropriate roles for the laity in the governance of their church.

Call to Action Conference

Perhaps much of the episcopal and institutional resistance and opposition to the Boston-based Voice of the Faithful—which we will examine later in this chapter—can be traced to a remarkable church event that occurred three decades earlier. In 1974, the National Conference of Catholic Bishops (now the U.S. Conference of Catholic Bishops) determined to mark the United States' celebration of its bicentennial anniversary by holding a "Call to Action Conference" in October 1976. The theme of the conference—a respectful nod to the American pledge of allegiance to the flag—was "Liberty and Justice for All": two values, it should be remembered, which were implicitly and explicitly affirmed by the Second Vatican Council.

Under the leadership of Cardinal John Dearden, archbishop of Detroit and NCCB president, the conference planners called for seven episcopal consultations similar to congressional hearings to be held throughout the country in the eighteen months prior to the conference. Panels of bishops listened to the views and concerns of over five hundred persons. The bishops also considered eight thousand written reflections and recommendations from dioceses, parishes, and Catholic organizations from nearly half of the nations' dioceses, which led in turn to eight working documents for the Call to Action Conference. The conference itself was comprised of nine delegates from each of the 167 dioceses (152 dioceses were represented) who were appointed by the bishop. The delegates included 100 bishops and 92 delegates from various national organizations which were each allotted one delegate. The assembled delegates totaled 1,340. Only the 92 delegates representing national organizations were not appointed by bishops. The cards were stacked, it would seem, for a moderate to conservative outcome. In the words of the publication *A.D. 1977*, issued by the Quixote Center of Hyattsville, Maryland (from which this review of the Call to Action Conference relies): "It was not a group that expected great happenings. How mistaken the skeptics were to be!"

The recommendations made by the CTA Conference sound remarkably similar to calls for renewal and reform in the first years of the twenty-first century. The conference recommended:

> That church authorities on all levels . . . hold themselves account-
> able to the people of God for their financial policies and practices . . .
> Parish and diocesan pastoral councils should be established and share
> responsibilities with their pastors and bishops. . . . That a National
> Review Board, composed of members of the church (bishops, clergy,
> religious and laity) be established to address itself aggressively to the
> issue of due process. . . . That the local church must be involved in

the selection of bishops and pastors. . . . That the National Conference of Bishops take affirmative action to respectfully petition the
Holy Father . . . to allow married men to be ordained to the priesthood . . . and to allow priests to exercise the right to marry and remain in or resume the active priesthood (*A.D. 1977* as quoted in
Leonard Swidler's foreword, "Not Resignation, But Creative Action,"
to Heinrich Fries's *Suffering from the Church*).

Some recommendations were mild in light of current church
practice. For example, that female children be granted the right
and opportunity to serve at the altar, that sexist language be
eliminated from church documents, and that the bishops "pro-
mote the full participation of women in the life and ministry of
the church." Other recommendations were clearly progressive.
The conference delegates called upon the American bishops to "affirm more clearly the right and responsibility of married people to
form their own consciences and to discern what is morally appropriate within the context of their marriage. [And to] initiate dialogue with Rome . . . to allow women to be ordained to the
diaconate and priesthood."

Shortly after the CTA Conference concluded, Cardinal Dearden
reported to the bishops at their semiannual meeting in November
1976 that "in general the actions recommended to us indicate a re-
alism, an independence, and a critical and mature judgment remarkable in a first assembly conducted along democratic lines . . .
our response should make clear our continuing commitment to co-
responsibility" (quoted in *Suffering from the Church*).

Hardly had Dearden spoken these words when the door was
slammed on the conference's recommendations. Moreover, conservative church authorities mounted a sustained effort to restore
the church to its pre-conciliar status. A restorationist agenda, it is
now acknowledged, has controlled church life from the last years
of the 1970s to the present. It explains why the institutional church
has failed to embrace Cardinal Joseph Bernardin's Common Ground
Initiative and remains resistant to and fearful of organizations and
movements that emerged in the spirit of Dearden's Call To Action

Conference—organizations like Call To Action (which continues the vision of the original conference with annual conventions), Women's Ordination Conference, and FutureChurch. Even as moderate and centrist an organization as Voice of the Faithful has met with inflexible resistance from many bishops and pastors.

Voice of the Faithful

Possessing faith that dared to speak, Voice of the Faithful emerged in the Archdiocese of Boston when a few adult Catholics understood they bore a responsibility to address the clergy abuse scandals brought into high relief by reports that Boston priest John Geoghan had molested more than 130 children in a half-dozen parishes over some three decades. While the scandal shocked the sensibilities of Boston's large Catholic community, it motivated some to take action. Cardiologist and Nobel laureate Dr. James Muller approached his pastor, Fr. Thomas Powers of Saint John's parish in Wellesley, about the possibility of starting a discussion group. In the company of two longtime friends, John and Mary Riley, Muller raised the idea with Powers after Sunday Mass in early February 2002. What followed is a series of faithful, daring decisions and initiatives that signal the coming of age of American Catholics. James Muller dared to approach his pastor; Tom Powers dared to trust the wisdom and goodness of his parishioners; women and men dared to stand and speak when their pastor invited them to remain after Sunday Mass to discuss the abuse scandal.

Powers, exhibiting keen pastoral insight, sat off to the side, letting Muller and parishioner Tom Smith lead the discussion. Muller began, "I want to thank Father Powers for giving us this opportunity to discuss the terrible crisis in our church. I have found it very confusing and distressing. I suspect many of you feel the same way. We thought it might be useful to share our reactions to the revelations that are occurring." With this simple, unpretentious invitation extended by a fellow parishioner to discuss the crisis welling up in the church, a local community gave the Spirit room to do what the Spirit does—to inspire hope and resolve where confusion and discouragement hold forth. Parishioners had been treated as adults—and responded as adults. Later, meetings were held in the basement meeting room of Saint John's church, meetings that evolved into a national organization of 33,000 Catholics—33,000 *adult* Catholics.

The genesis of Voice of the Faithful is narrated by James Muller and Charles Kenny in their 2004 book *Keep the Faith, Change the Church*. Their story captures in verbatim exchanges between archdiocesan officials and VOTF leaders the defensiveness, secrecy, and clerical attitudes that have compounded the suffering of abuse victims and their families. In the pages that follow we examine why VOTF has generated such unusual anxiety in reactionary Catholics and church authorities as well as explicit hostility from numerous bishops.

The goals of VOTF are succinct and clear, although the third goal, as we shall see, is judged by some to be fraught with ambiguity. First, VOTF wants to offer support to victims of clergy sexual abuse; second, they desire to affirm "priests of integrity;" and third, they call for reform of church structures that no longer support the vitality and mission of the church. The heart of the first goal is compassion, the second is encouragement of the large majority of priests who have not betrayed the trust of children and teenagers.

So far, so good. It makes no sense to be threatened by a commitment to acts of compassion and encouragement. Perhaps the institutional church believes it is doing quite well in responding pastorally and compassionately to the thousands of victims and victim-survivors of sexual abuse. Perhaps, too, the institutional church sees an implied criticism in the first goal of VOTF. Even some bishops have acknowledged they have not done enough by way of pastoral response to abuse victims. Can compassionate outreach from the laity to their wounded sisters and brothers actually be a source of discomfort to them? The second goal, encouragement and support for "priests of integrity" should hardly prompt concern from the bishops. They have repeatedly and publicly affirmed priests who labor faithfully and tirelessly through dark nights of plummeting morale and spiraling suspicion and mistrust. Do some bishops suspect that VOTF's second goal is a subtle attempt on the part of parishioners to turn the loyalty of priests away from their bishop and to the laity? Perhaps a few rather paranoid bishops might feel this way, but it is far more likely that the vast majority of bishops and church officials welcome and endorse the first two goals of VOTF.

It is likely the third goal, the call for reform of church structures, that is the source of so much fear and anxiety on the part of many church leaders toward VOTF. Yet, reform of the church should hardly be threatening if we understand the church to be *semper reformanda*—always in need of reform and renewal. Such has it been throughout its two-thousand-year history and so will it be for ages to come. VOTF, moreover, is calling for reform of structures that no longer serve the communal life of the faithful and the mission of the church. It is not calling for doctrinal reform. Structural reform and renewal are essential for living, organic communities of faithful disciples. The very history of the church makes that abundantly clear.

What is going on here? we might ask. I propose the real issue church officials have with VOTF's third goal is control and power. Consider the exchange reported in *Keep the Faith, Change the Church* between VOTF leaders Muller, Mary Scanlon Calcaterra, and Steve Krueger in their meeting with archdiocesan officials Bishop Walter Edyvean and Father Mark O'Connell. Muller asks Bishop Edyvean, "We've heard that you're blocking us in parishes, that you're calling pastors and telling them not to let Voice of the Faithful meet on church property. Are you blocking us?"

Edyvean replies, "There are a lot of issues we have with your organization. We have to know what you're about." *We have to know what you're about* tips his hand. These are words of control. They say in effect, "We are in charge here, we are in control." What is behind such assertions of authority? Laity coming together to discuss a crisis in the church and then organizing with stated goals and financial resources are perceived as a threat to church leaders. So threatened, they feel compelled to know "what they are about." When confronted by this form of control, the laity might well respond, "Of course you have to know what we're about. But we members of the faithful have a right to know what you, our church leaders, are about. We are all in this together and the church we love is in serious trouble."

From the beginning, VOTF was met with suspicion—and aggressive resistance. The question returns: "What is going on here?" A group of educated, liberated, adult Catholics are rightly distressed and disturbed by arguably the worst scandal and crisis ever to engulf the U.S. Catholic church. They are middle-aged, moderate, loyal parishioners, most in the grandparent, even great-grandparent age cohort, taking seriously what Vatican II told them about their responsibility to address important issues affecting the life and mission of the church. They organize as is their right—and their numbers and resolve provide them with what many church authorities fear in the hands of others: power.

From a feudal perspective, the anxious concern of Bishop Edyvean and Father O'Connell is understandable. The serfs were organizing. From the vision of church proposed by Pius X, it is predictable, for in the eyes of Edyvean and his archbishop, their responsibility for governance and control was being threatened. From the perspective of the leaders of VOTF, on the other hand, Catholics were taking responsible action to address a crisis of unprecedented weight. They were in the church's service. They were, nevertheless, criticized well beyond the chancery of the Archdiocese of Boston. David O'Brien of Holy Cross College writes: "Even supporters of a stronger lay voice seem quick to criticize VOTF, worrying that its support for 'structural change' and its democratic spirit might lead down a slippery slope to Unitarianism. That suspicion shows little confidence in the intelligence or commitment of ordinary Catholics" (*Commonweal*, February 14, 2003).

There is something sad, even tragic in a minor key, about the institutional church's reaction to VOTF. We can imagine another response from the archdiocesan officials in Boston and other bishops throughout the country, a response inspired by the gospel and the conciliar documents. What if the archbishop of Boston and his episcopal colleagues had expressed words of support and encouragement to the leaders of VOTF? What would have happened if bishops urged their pastors to support and encourage VOTF? What if U.S. bishops had invited these lay leaders to sit down with them? What would have happened had bishops listened non-defensively to these educated, articulate lay leaders? Were not the goals of VOTF, all three of them, goals of the bishops themselves? Even the third goal ought to be embraced by the bishops—at least in theory. It is simply one expression of a finite church's need for ongoing renewal and reform under the inspiration of the Spirit. A graced moment was lost. An opportunity for solidarity and renewal was allowed to slip by. Sadly, many bishops turned sister and brother allies into adversaries. Victims of abuse are poorer for it, the laity are poorer for it, priests are poorer for it, bishops are poorer for it—the church itself is poorer for it.

The National Review Board: A Voice of the Faithful

A blanket of rain clouds held low over the Cleveland airport as I caught an early morning flight to Washington, D.C. Robert Bennett, head of the research committee of the National Review Board for the Protection of Children and Young People, had invited me to meet with a number of the board and their staff. On the top floor of his law offices next to the White House, I sat across an imposing, oversized marble conference table from review board members Bennett, Jane Chiles, Nicholas Cafardi, and their staff attorneys. To my right was a court stenographer. A three-hour "friendly deposition" (as I came to think of the meeting) began with minimal formality. The interviewers had done their homework. Their questions were not only germane to the abuse crisis, they reflected an awareness of the structural factors at work—clericalism, secrecy, denial, a pervasive, unquestioning loyalty to the system.

Waiting for my late afternoon flight back to Cleveland, I sensed the board would fulfill its mandate and let the chips fall where they may. There was no question but that they would dare to report what they had learned. And so they did. While certain aspects of the report, in my judgment, missed the mark—its conclusion, for example, that "the current crisis at heart is one of faith and morality"—the board did not blink from criticizing the bishops themselves and church systems and structures of governance that contributed to the abuse scandal. This was no mean accomplishment.

The board issued its report, we noted in chapter 5, on February 27, 2004. On that day the U.S. church and the American public heard a voice of the faithful expressed with unusual passion and conviction. At a press conference marking the release of the board's comprehensive and careful study, Robert Bennett's voice became a voice *for* the faithful heard from coast to coast and in many parts of the world. The symbolic import of the press conference was its sub-theme: the emerging role of the laity. This too was the church. Not only men in black suits but baptized disciples, men and women, parents and grandparents, whose commitment to the gospel and love of the church were both evident and unquestioned.

The existence of the National Review Board is in itself significant. Never before had bishops commissioned lay men and women to study a problem involving bishops and priests and to make a public report of their findings. Moreover, the bishops provided the funds necessary to complete the study which were considerable in spite of the board members' *pro bono* investment of their time and talent. It is right, I believe, to note that the leadership of the bishops' conference took this unprecedented step under great duress and incredible pressure to take definitive action to protect children and young people. Never before had the American bishops been so strongly and publicly criticized by society at large, by the media, by the judiciary, by victims and victim support groups, by their priests, and by the Catholic laity. As they gathered in Dallas for their June 2002 semiannual meeting, their credibility as moral leaders and their status as episcopal pastors had dropped to an all time low. The decision to create the National Review Board was made, one could argue, less from genuine trust in the laity's wisdom and competence than from sheer necessity— nothing less than such an unprecedented step would turn the tide of anger and criticism directed at the bishops. While the motivation for creating the board may have been less than ideal, the decision to do so should be applauded.

The following findings of the report suggest structural changes in the church and point to episcopal attitudes that distance bishops from the faithful. The first two underscore the harm that results from bishops' suspicion and mistrust of the laity.

- Many church leaders refused to meet with victim support groups because they disagreed with the agendas of some of these groups. Although some members of victim support groups are not always fair to the bishops and are unwilling to give credit where it is due, disregarding these groups is short-sighted and contributes to the perception of a closed and secretive church. Distaste for the messenger too often blinded church leadership to the significance of the message (IV, B, 2).
- [I]t was reported to the Review Board that the response of one bishop to the suggested adoption of the Five Principles in 1992 (for dealing with reports of clergy abuse) was: "No one is going to tell me how to run my diocese." We do not know what the reaction of his fellow bishops was to this statement, but we hope that, should such a statement be made today, the other bishops would correct such myopia by telling the bishop that no one, not even a bishop, has the right to risk the well-being of youngsters entrusted to his care; nor does he have the right to risk the good name of his fellow bishops and the entire church in the United States by his intransigence (IV, B, 8, d).
- The process for selecting bishops should include meaningful lay consultation (V, D).

- The bishops and other church leaders must listen to and be responsive to the concerns of the laity. To accomplish this, the hierarchy must act with less secrecy, more transparency, and a greater openness to the gifts that all members of the church bring to her (V, F).

The review board's report, read in its entirety, supports the brave voices of the laity that are rising in the midst of the current storm. What the bishops have withheld—support and encouragement—the report has extended.

Accountability of the Bishops

In spite of the enormous good accomplished by the work of the review board, considerable anger remains directed at the bishops. Catholics see a double standard for bishops: zero tolerance for priests accused of sexual abuse but only fraternal correction for bishops who have reassigned abuser clerics. (Rather than zero tolerance, the goal of both bishops and laity should be *zero risk* as far as humanly possible.) Nowhere has this anger been better captured than in Bishop Thomas Gumbleton's October 10, 2003, letter to the editors of *Commonweal* magazine:

Bishops like [Rembert] Weakland, Bernard Law, and many others who were guilty of grave mistakes, and even criminal actions, still function publicly. On the other hand, priests sometimes guilty of far less grave actions, some of which were single incidents and many years ago, are forced to resign, are not allowed to publicly celebrate Mass, or even to appear in clerical attire. "Zero tolerance" has been the cruel response rendered to priests by the bishops, while bishops escape such penalties even though it was they who constantly hid the grave problems by secretly moving guilty priests from one place to another.

Both Archbishop Weakland and Cardinal Law, we see now, took action supported by the feudal structures examined in chapter one. Weakland used the financial resources of his benefice, the

Archdiocese of Milwaukee, in an attempt to avoid scandal and the personal embarrassment of his romantic involvement with an adult who befriended him. Law, also in an attempt to avoid scandal and to protect the reputation and power of the institutional church, transferred abuser priests to unsuspecting parishes thereby enabling them to continue their criminal seductions. Both prelates exercised something akin to feudal control over the finances of their archdioceses and their clergy personnel. Both were motivated by the threat of scandal. Sadly—and tragically—both compounded scandal in their secretive attempts to avoid scandal.

Until the bishops go beyond the "fraternal correction" urged by the review board report, the skepticism and anger of many Catholics will hold strong. Gumbleton went on to say in his *Commonweal* letter: "I have found that nothing causes greater anger on the part of laypeople and greater loss of credibility in episcopal leadership than this double standard. We can only hope that Voice of the Faithful and other lay groups will have the stamina to persist in their efforts to hold the bishops accountable and to bring structural reform to the church."

What is hopeful is that VOTF is first holding themselves accountable as adult Catholics. They sense their very integrity is at stake. As they continue to "speak the truth in love," they show every sign of fulfilling Bishop Gumbleton's hope.

Adsum

Voice of the Faithful members, other lay groups, and Catholics in general claim and hold steadfast to a long-honored tenant of their faith: fidelity first to their conscience as enlightened by the gospel. They understand that Cardinal John Henry Newman's famous axiom, "Conscience first, Pope afterwards," is not meant to pit them against the voice of the teaching church but to remind them of their status as adult disciples of Jesus. They are in ever greater numbers standing humbly but firmly in the assembly of believers and saying, "*Adsum*. I am present and I pledge my loyalty to the gospel, to my conscience, and to the church." They take heart and courage from the words of John Paul II:

> Conscience . . . is the "place" where man is illuminated by a light which does not come to him from his created and always fallible reason, but from the very Wisdom of the Word in whom all things were created. "Conscience," as Vatican II again admirably states, "is a man's secret core, and his sanctuary. There he is alone with God whose voice echoes in his depths ("Truth in the Magisterium," Address to the Second International Congress on Moral Theology, *The Pope Speaks*, 34, 2, 1989).

This adult pledge of loyalty to gospel, conscience, and church is not made lightly. The responsibilities implicit in adult discipleship sooner or later require considerable moral courage. When one dares to speak, criticism is sure to follow. But a lesson has been learned in the early years of the twenty-first century—criticism from the institutional church pales in comparison to the criticism of conscience. Lay men and women continue to see signs of hope and to hear words of encouragement from their sisters and brothers, from their pastors, and from a number of bishops.

Consider the counsel of Cardinal Walter Kasper:

> We follow church leaders only to the extent that they themselves follow Christ. . . . Some situations oblige one to obey God and one's own conscience rather than the leaders of the church. Indeed, one may even be obliged to accept excommunication rather than act against one's own conscience (*Leadership in the Church*).

Cardinal Kasper, standing in the tradition of Cardinal Newman, dares to say in fresh language what has always sustained the church in times of crisis. Our first fidelity must be to Christ and our conscience. The Voice of the Faithful and a growing number of groups calling for renewal and reform are speaking from the center of their souls—what is heard is the voice of conscience.

CHAPTER SEVEN

CONTEMPLATIVE CONVERSATION

One who loves God necessarily loves silence.

—Thomas Merton

The Christian of the future will be a mystic or he will not exist at all.

—Karl Rahner

We have to earn silence . . . to work for it: to make it not an absence but a presence; not emptiness but repletion. Silence is something more than just a pause; it is that enchanted place where space is cleared and time is stayed and the horizon itself expands.

—Pico Iyer

IF THIS IS INDEED A MOMENT in the church's history when one must dare to speak, it is certainly a moment when one must learn to be still, when one must learn to sit still. "All the evil in the world," wrote Blaise Pascal, "can be traced to our inability to sit still in a room." Pascal's maxim holds an important lesson for us at this critical juncture in the church's life. Our conversation will be beneficial and life-giving to the extent that it flows out of silence and leads in turn back to silence. And that is no easy task in a culture that abhors silence. We are a people who cannot even take a walk in the woods without a cell phone pressed to our ear or drive to work without the radio or a compact disk filling the cell-like space of our car. Silence has become for so many of us unsettling, disturbing—something profoundly awkward.

But silence that unmasks the soul's emptiness and lack of depth is potentially the same silence that holds the promise and power to let us see with the eyes of the heart and to listen with a spirit of compassion. Only in silence can we discover how to speak the truth in love and how to listen to others without filtering their words through our self-imposed screens of orthodoxy. It is in silence that we learn to embrace "the grace of self-doubt." It is in silence that we learn how to speak words that invite consideration and reflection. It is in silence that we learn how to dismantle our self-constructed defenses that buttress the historically conditioned structures of church governance. And it is in silence that we are led to intellectual and attitudinal conversion which allows true conversation to occur.

Both *conversion* and *conversation* are cognates of *converse*—to turn around, to turn toward another. Understood as a noun, *converse* includes the meaning of free and honest interchange of ideas, dreams, hopes—and, yes, fears. If we are to move beyond the polarizing ecclesial tensions now dividing progressives from conservatives and reactionaries from radical liberals, we need to examine the fears that breed mistrust and suspicion. What is it that we fear will be lost? If we can name these fears, we come to see that our fears have something in common—the loss of something understood as vital and essential to the life and mission of the church. Conservatives fear a loss of grounding, that somehow we are losing our lifeline to the tradition that holds us in communion with our ancestors in faith. They fear we are being co-opted by a secular, postmodern culture and in the process becoming shallow, banal, and, worst of all, relevant. Meanwhile, progressives fear we are losing the vitality and flexibility essential to a church that is organic and thoroughly rooted in history—that we are confusing uniformity with true unity. They see an institutional church that has become, for some sometime now, static, controlling, authoritarian, and triumphalistic.

Both conservatives and progressives fear that we are suffering the loss of our identity as God's faithful, pilgrim people. Instead of naming and owning their fears, both groups tend to assert with the confidence of religious conviction, the righteousness of their positions. "The grace of self doubt" is rejected as a capitulation to deep and enduring faith. In church circles as well as in the secular realm, fear and insecurity give birth to ideology. The ideologues in both groups need the voice and perspective of the other. Convinced of their theological rectitude, they move quickly to shrill argument and righteous declarations rather than turning first to the silence that prompts openness of heart and nudges the soul toward the place where conversion of intellect and imagination occur. The battle is joined and the first victims are humble listening and measured speech.

Contemplative conversation, conversation that emerges from silence and prayer, on the other hand, possesses a tone and humility that disarms defensive postures of rectitude. There is a freshness, a lightness of spirit present when this kind of conversation is entered into. No matter how neuralgic the subject under discussion—the nature of the church, its structures and disciplines—a true openness to the ideas and opinions of the dialogue partners is now perceptible. When such a spirit is absent, we inevitably bear witness to the clash of ideologies. And ideologies that take the shape of religious convictions are the meanest, most spirit-killing ideologies of all. I employ the term *ideology* here as a set of convictions and values that by nature are resistant to critical evaluation and assessment. Ideologies, because they lack "the grace of self doubt," are open only to the exposition and refinement of their emphatic declarations. Again and again history reminds us that ideologies cloaked in religious belief are not only spirit-killing but arguably the cause of more human bloodshed than secular, political, and economic ideologies.

Our best chance to move beyond the closed-mindedness that marks much of contemporary church discourse is to turn to the insights and wisdom of the church's contemplative tradition.

The Idol of Truth

It seems that many if not most of the acrimonious public exchanges between the commentators and writers representing both the conservative and progressive camps are so uncompromising is that both parties are convinced they are defending the truth of Christianity and Catholicism. Without disparaging the essential, critical role that revealed truth holds in the life and mission of the church, the message of Jesus is grounded in a scandalous communion of love between God and God's beloved creation—especially between God and God's beloved sons and daughters.

We seem to imagine that Jesus said, "I have come to bring you this great dogma, this great concept, and your salvation depends on understanding it correctly." Rather, the core of Christianity, as the church's contemplative and mystical traditions remind us, is the reality of new life, God's own life. The loving unity of this communal life, we have come to understand, is at the heart of Jesus' revelation and teaching. Because of this sacred revelation and teaching we know the sacred story of God's action in our lives. But our contemplative and mystical traditions won't let us forget that God is ultimately mystery and we know far less about God than we sometimes think. Do we really believe that we know the truth about God, the truth about the Spirit of God, the truth about grace and redemption? Do we believe, on a completely different and subservient level, that we know precisely what structures best serve the vitality and mission of the church in any given period of history? Some of us apparently do. And we cannot tolerate any doubt about our convictions whatsoever. When this happens, we make idols of our ideologies masking them as theological givens.

Perhaps it is the nature of religious conviction and belief that we assume a defensive, superior posture not only against other religious traditions but also against fellow believers who embrace our common faith from different perspectives. It is precisely against this faulty religious fidelity that the prophets of all ages speak out so strongly. The prophets of old understood more clearly than we do today that the most blinding fault of the true believer is always idolatry—making a historically conditioned understanding of God's mysterious ways into immutable truths that stand in no need whatsoever of further plumbing and reflection. We seem to have reached a stage of hardened polarization where civil conversation is all but impossible. In its place we have, on some sad occasions, faithful "idolators" screaming anathemas—self-appointed guardians of the true faith fighting for religious concepts dressed as immutable truths.

What is so striking about the present cultural wars engaging many of the developed Euro-American countries is that they are only minimally doctrinal in nature if doctrinal at all—understanding doctrine here as revealed teachings. More often than not, the matters so fiercely contested are about church structures, ecclesiastical disciplines, the role of the laity, and the hot-button issues of accountability, transparency, and governance. What is at stake, it should be clear, is not revealed truth but long-standing lines of control and power.

Silences

There are, of course, unholy silences. At some length, we examined unholy silences in a previous book, *Sacred Silence: Denial and the Crisis in the Church*. Perhaps most unholy of all, it was proposed, is the silence of denial. The silence that holds us bound to our ego-selves out of fear and cowardice is the opposite of the silence that leads to contemplative openness. Here in this pseudo-quiet the soul betrays its integrity and purity out of fear that it will displease those in authority, that it will suffer criticism, that it will jeopardize the faint pleasure of acceptance. Unholy silence leads not to soulfulness but to restlessness. It is here that paranoia takes root and suspicion takes hold. In this dark silence those who disagree or differ are demonized. Out of this silence conversation is impossible. Only bullet-words of self-righteous certitudes are aimed at those who differ or disagree.

Without denying the reality of certain tensions and problems, others embrace a silence designed to keep them from entering the fray. Things are not as they should be, they admit to themselves, but they remain silent. Let others take the necessary steps to address issues and structures begging for attention and reform. Terrible things happen, we acknowledge as part of our cultural wisdom, when good men and women simply do nothing, say nothing, in times of crisis. The silence of indifference can make cowards of us all. It puts not only the church at profound risk but our society as well. Surely the vast numbers of citizens that remain silent instead of exercising their responsibility to vote threaten the very fabric of democracy. Silence remains one of the great sins of omission.

Victim survivors of sexual abuse know a different kind of silence. Often too young to find the words to report their private horrors they dwell in a land of silence and darkness. For years they endure their personal agony wrapped in shrouds of hopelessness and helplessness. Instead of a silence leading to insight and compassion, their dark solitude takes them to the edge of despair and for some, tragically, to the despair that chooses self-annihilation.

We are not good, I believe, at preserving the personal silence that feeds our souls. In a culture that rewards feverish striving and perceives life as a race that goes to the swift and the driven, silence is dismissed as an unnecessary and dangerous luxury. For many it is worse than a frivolous luxury, it is a mask for laziness. The great mystics and contemplatives of every age offer us moderns another perspective. They remind us that it is in silence that we come to terms with our own limitations. They teach us that in stillness we sense our unity with our ancestors and with all who have gone before us. It is in silence that our imaginations begin to stir and new horizons come into view. In silence we catch a glimpse of the truth in those with whom we disagree.

Like all things good and necessary, there is a danger in silence. We can allow wounds to fester as we sit in silence. Silence can nurture old animosities and stoke embers of unresolved anger. But the risk must be taken. For silence is the safest route to that point of inner conversion that permits authentic conversation. And whenever we find common ground for authentic conversation we find a communion of silences preparing the way. When individuals and groups address the present crisis out of their respective silences their words invite conversation rather than conflict—they reflect the grace of self-doubt.

The silence that gives birth to contemplative conversation is the same silence that inspires effective preaching. We have come to understand in recent years the need for a period of silence following effective preaching. There is a similar need for silence whenever we engage in honest and humble conversation. This instinctive pull toward an inward stillness signals that the words spoken and heard were authentic. Surely, times of crisis require inspired words and inspired deeds. They also require silence that leads to wisdom born of solitude.

Contemplative Consciousness

Poet and statesman Vaclav Havel, a leader of the Velvet Revolution that liberated Czechoslovakia from Soviet domination, understood the critical importance of consciousness raising in any effort to bring about meaningful change in society and government. In a speech delivered to a joint meeting of the U.S. Congress, the then president of the Czech Republic, said that

> [T]he salvation of this human world lies nowhere else than in the human heart, in the human power to reflect, in human meekness and in human responsibility. Without a global revolution in . . . human consciousness, nothing will change for the better, and the catastrophe toward which this world is headed . . . will be unavoidable (*Time*, March 5, 1990).

The raising of consciousness, Havel reminds us, is fundamental and essential for any sustained change in human behavior and the structures of society.

Scripture scholar Walter Brueggemann provides helpful examples of the shaping power of consciousness from his study and analysis of the kings of Israel in his classic *The Prophetic Imagination*. In contrast to the kings' and other elites' "royal consciousness," a consciousness of preferment and entitlement resulting from their ascendancy to leadership of the people, Moses shaped and formed an "alternative consciousness" in the minds and hearts of the people he led out of exile into freedom. In the alternative consciousness fostered by Moses, God does indeed have a preferential option for the oppressed and those living on the margins of society. God is here understood as a God of compassion and justice who will liberate the oppressed—a God who now sustains and nourishes his people. Royal consciousness, the consciousness of those in power, inevitably comes to see reality from the perspective of privilege, affluence, and the survival and strengthening of the social order and institutions that are intrinsically linked to their station in life. It is a consciousness out of touch with the lived realities—the struggles and joys—of those outside the circle of the elite. And it fails to understand the common aspirations and anxieties of ordinary people. In its extreme form it leads to crass insensitivity, even deafness, to the cries of the oppressed and the poor; an attitude expressed succinctly in Marie Antoinette's "Let them eat cake." In the jargon of today, those constricted by royal consciousness, "just don't get it."

There is present in some church authorities, we noted in chapter 4, a form of royal consciousness that inhibits their ability to understand and to identify with the laity's experience of everyday life and their experience of church. These men live in their own encapsulated, ecclesial world. We find here, not surprisingly, the breeding ground of clericalism and the alienating arrogance common in clerics who have taken too seriously their ordained status. For these church leaders a spontaneous suspicion and mistrust develops toward those who do not share in their ecclesial status and authority, especially when disagreement is expressed or action is taken.

It may be helpful to consider briefly the implications of "clerical/episcopal consciousness" as a form of "royal consciousness." Here, understandably enough, the focus is on governance, order, unity, and orthodoxy. What can be lost is a sense of common ground, of mutuality with the baptized, the conviction that the Spirit is moving through the whole people of God. From the mindset of royal consciousness it is easy, even natural, to lose the perspective of the faithful. The view from an "alternative consciousness" is quite different. Those outside the inner ecclesial circle cope with a fair amount of frustration. It is made clear that their experience of discipleship is not taken seriously by church officials. More, they feel mistrusted as less than full, equal, and adult members of the church.

Instead of either a royal or an alternative consciousness with their distinctive points of view and priorities, the present crisis is evoking a "disciple consciousness" common to all of the baptized. Here the good of the church and the mission of the church are embraced as a common responsibility. Though a common responsibility already exists in theory, it has been eclipsed by the sharp divide between clergy and laity. Within this common consciousness there will exist, however, two distinct manifestations of discipleship. In the communion of believers, those called to full-time ministry or ordained ministry or other charismatic ministries bear weighty responsibilities not always shared with the vast majority of believers. These ministers possess a "leader consciousness," a consciousness that does not, however, supercede their disciple consciousness. And while the majority of church members are outside the circle of recognized ecclesial ministry, they might develop a "partner consciousness" that remains grounded in their "discipleship consciousness." In refocusing Christian identity as foundationally linked to baptism, Vatican II implicitly called for the development of a common consciousness for the people of God. While this is a softening of the clergy/laity distinction, it is in harmony with the council's vision.

Contemplative Action

Around kitchen tables, at coffee stations in the work place, over drinks at cocktail parties, men and women are asking what can be done—more specifically what *can they do*—to address the unprecedented crisis rocking their church? They understand the pre-conciliar days of passive compliance practiced for centuries by

the laity are coming to an end. Owning their responsibility as
adult members of the church, they now see their very integrity is
at stake should they slip back into the comfortable, passive patterns of deference they once displayed toward their bishops and
pastors. Many have joined Voice of the Faithful and other renewal
organizations. Others have written letters to their bishops and
pastors, organized conferences and workshops addressing the scandal, reached out to abuse victims, supported their parish priests
toiling under clouds of suspicion and draining work-loads. Awakened as if from a long adolescent slumber, they now are alert to
the stirrings of the Spirit to meaningful action.

But how do they take action without falling into *activism*—action for action's sake? Orthodox theologian Alexander Schmemann
offers a word of advice:

> It its present situation, the church is a caricature of the world, with
> the difference that in the world, fights, institutions and so forth are
> real. In the church, they are illusory because they are not related to
> anything. For salvation, this fussy activism is not needed; for joy
> and peace in the Holy Spirit—not needed either. The question is,
> What is the Church needed for? This question must be asked by
> the church all the time, before any action. The church is the con-
> nection with Christ and the relation of everything to Christ. . . .
> Why talk about it? Let's start with money, or organizational prob-
> lems . . . then everything becomes pierced with a horrible clerical
> boredom (*The Journals of Father Alexander Schmemann*).

The present church crisis, of course, is indeed real and far more serious than "money or organizational problems." Still Schmemann's
insight holds. Why is the church so important to us? What is the
church needed for? Because it is our connection with Christ, it is essential that action follows upon prayer for the guidance of Christ's
Spirit and that it follows—especially from the perspective of this
chapter—from a contemplative silence.

The action of the laity, in this their moment, appears for the
most part to be *willing* rather than *willful*. This is a critical dis-

tinction for action that is contemplative in its origin and spirit—
the only kind of action that will revitalize and reform the church.
I draw here on the work of Gerald May in his 1982 book *Will and
Spirit*. Willfulness, he points out, no matter the righteousness,
correctness, or goodness of its intended object or goal, ultimately
betrays. For it is an exercise of will grounded in ego, mastery, and
control. Not even striving after something as noble as spiritual
growth or holiness or church reform can be forced. Willfulness by
definition lacks the grace of self-doubt. It springs forth from what
Thomas Merton identifies as the *false self*, our ego-self. Bernard
of Clairvaux saw the danger here. In his sermon "On the Search
for Wisdom," he enjoins his listeners, "Be converted and come.
Converted from what? From your own *willfulness*" (emphasis
added).

Willingness, on the other hand, emerges out of contemplative
silence, out of the humility that recognizes not even the best de-
sires of our hearts and minds can be forced. When our actions are
willful, we fall victim to the age-old trap of Semi-Pelagianism—
the belief that willpower alone is sufficient to achieve our spiritual objectives. When we act willingly, however, our actions are
grounded in trust and surrender. We intuitively understand that
we are ultimately not in control, that there is a divine plan or
order, and our supreme good is to be found in living and acting in
harmony with this divine ordering. Willing people act with purpose and resolve, but with a peace of soul that recognizes that
God's Spirit is the primary actor and source of all that is truly
good and right. They act with hope knowing that the Spirit has
promised never to abandon the church. They act with patience
knowing they must work through numerous frustrations and
failures before authentic renewal and reform are achieved.

Willful people, especially willful church people, act with a
gravity of soul that gives them away. There is no joy in their
hearts, no sense of humor, no lightness of being. It is as if they are
the only guardians of orthodoxy and truth and the church they
love is disintegrating before their eyes. And they are angry.

In a culture that celebrates the individual to the point of radical individualism, a willful stance toward life dominates western society. From the Nike mantra *just do it,* to the Army's recruiting slogan *be all you can be,* the individual, willful pursuit of our goals has become firmly lodged in our collective unconscious. A willing stance toward life and meaningful action is found only among individuals who have learned how to "sit still in a room," who have come to treasure their souls' thirst for contemplative silence. Interestingly, psychologists have discovered that optimal athletic performance flows out of the mindfulness and centeredness associated with a willing rather than a willful exercise of will. Willing, as distinct from willful, athletes compete with a certain relaxed, yet focused awareness. Trusting in their talent and instincts, these athletes are less likely to press— and more likely to perform consistently at their optimal level. Willful athletes, on the other hand, believe they can perform on a higher level than their present statistics indicate and *will* themselves to do so. Their strained and tense efforts more often than not disappoint them. So it will be with the church. Believers who speak and act willingly, out of contemplative silence, out of the grace of self-doubt, will contribute greatly to the healing and renewal of our church. Those who speak and act willfully—no matter the righteousness of their purpose—will grow ever more frustrated and angry.

Contemplative Power

The wisdom of the street holds that the only way to deal with power is to deal from power. Or from a more adversarial perspective—the only way to fight power is with power. It is not only the wisdom of the street, it is a lesson of history itself. We confronted the power of Great Britain with the power of a revolutionary army. We confronted the military powers of totalitarian regimes with the allied armies of democratic nations. We confronted the power of management with the power of the union. And this kind of logic demands we confront the abuses of church power with the power of protest and strategy.

In the present critical situation facing the church, the faithful search for appropriate and effective ways to engage structures and powers of a strongly entrenched institution. Otherwise, we risk disunity and even schism. Might we not learn from the exercise of power in Jesus' life and ministry? It is a function of power indeed, but a power essentially different from political and military power. And it arose out of Jesus' contemplative heart and his communion with the God he professed and the Spirit he embodied. Jesus' prophetic, social, and healing power, grounded in his authoritative way of life and teaching, moved the hearts of the *laos*—the people—and made anxious and fearful those who held both political and religious power in his day. He dwelt among us to courageously bear witness to a new order grounded in the Creator's embrace of and love for all of humanity.

At the heart of Jesus' preaching is a fundamental equality and dignity for all members of the human family that rang true in the hearts of those who heard him. Those who speak today for the vitality and mission of the church must likewise ring true. Their courage and fire must be rooted in the courage and fire of the Spirit. Only thus rooted can they speak and act in the spirit of Jesus' own power.

In previous chapters we have, in fact, explored various uses of power to bring about a renewed and reformed church. There is power indeed in holding faithfully to the vision of church taught by the Second Vatican Council. There is power indeed in daring to speak from our convictions and experiences as faithful disciples. There is power in giving expression to our questions welling up from our love and faith. There is power in standing in the assembly and declaring one's presence as an adult member of the church. There is power in holding church leaders accountable for their decisions and malfeasance and in demanding transparency in place of secrecy. There is power in organizing so that voices might be heard and action steps discerned.

Against all odds? Perhaps. The outcome of courageous speech and contemplative conversation is unclear in the short run, obscured by the fears of the power elite and by the self-imposed horizons of church leaders. But the short run, while important in its own right, really should not overly matter. In the grand scheme of things, the truth will out and the Spirit will guide and sustain the church through the worst of times. It is critically important, therefore, that we speak our truth in love and act with courage and humility even when our words and deeds seem to be fruitless.

Hope rests, in the long run, in God's promise of fidelity to the ecclesial community of disciples. Otherwise our words and deeds will simply be another exercise of power confronting power. When that happens the possibility of contemplative conversation—the only kind of conversation that allows for the wisdom of the Spirit—is lost. And with it the realization of authentic renewal and reformation is delayed.

CHAPTER EIGHT

A RISING CHORUS

To sin by silence when they should protest, makes cowards of human beings.

—Abraham Lincoln

[Jesus] put his fingers into the man's ears and spitting, touched his tongue; then he looked up to heaven and emitted a groan. He said to him, *"Ephphata!"* (that is, "Be opened!") At once the man's ears were opened; he was freed from the impediment, and he began to speak plainly.

—Mark 7:33-35

Desire is to love as belief is to faith: each is a means to an end; each is so easily mistaken for the end.

—Fenton Johnson

"WHAT ARE WE AFRAID OF?" I began *Sacred Silence: Denial and the Crisis in the Church* with this very question. What, indeed, are we so afraid of? The answers, I trust, are suggested in the text and subtext of the chapters of this book. We are afraid of honest conversation, honest dialogue, honest questions because they may take us where we do not want to go. Because they may displease religious authorities who still do not understand that the Spirit inspires where and when and in whom it wills. Because feudal structures remain indifferent at best to the voices of ordinary folks. Because we still do not trust the common ground that unites us as believers and disciples. In ecclesial crises, we have seen, it is necessary to honor and reverence the community's tradition while

equally honoring and reverencing the presence of the Spirit calling the community forth as a living and organic reality. The tension undergirding these twin fidelities is considerable.

"Be careful with words," urged Elie Wiesel, "they're dangerous. Be wary of them. They beget either demons or angels" *(Leg-
ends of Our Time)*. Daring to speak in crisis moments such as the
church is experiencing now, therefore, means taking the risk that
our speech may do more harm than good. No matter the danger, a
far greater danger awaits us if we fail to speak the truth in love.

This is the time, I have argued, for faithful Catholics, lay and
clergy, to speak candidly from the contemplative silence of their
hearts, from their center, if you will. I say this aware of Kathleen
Norris's warning about what happens when we speak or write from
our center. "[W]hen we write from the center . . . when we write
about what matters to us most, words will take us places we don't
want to go. You begin to see that you will have to say things you
don't want to say, that may even be dangerous to say, but are ab-
solutely necessary" *(Amazing Grace: A Vocabulary of Faith)*. For
the good of the church, and for the sake of our own integrity, it is ab-
solutely necessary for us to speak, to question, and to listen. Countless Catholics have already done so and some, as we have seen, have
suffered for it. In spite of attempts to silence various voices of the
faithful, in spite of attempts to keep them from assembling on parish
properties, in spite of warnings from chanceries, a chorus of faithful
voices is heard growing ever more strong and confident. The voices
rise from all quarters of the church: some weak, some strong, sometimes in harmony, sometimes off key. Sometimes the lyrics move us
to tears, sometimes to action. As if with one mind, the chorus understands that silence is no longer an option.

In this final chapter, we listen for the grace-notes that point
us in the right direction, for grace-notes that give us hope and
courage. These glimpses of grace are manifestations of the divine
presence abiding with us in the midst of our own darkness and
discouragement. We "catch" them in honest, humble words spoken, written, and sometimes sung. We discover them in the word-

less example of the exploited and wounded who carry on as faithful disciples. We hear them in the cries of children and women who suffer abuse. We see them in the eyes of tired parents trying to hold their families together in the midst of a soulless culture. Together, in less than perfect harmony, they make up a rising chorus of the people's faith.

Realistic Hope

In recent years we've discovered where the "vocations" have gone. I speak here of vocations to the priesthood and religious life. They are to be found, to a large extent, on our college campuses and in our graduate schools of theology and ministry. A major segment of my ministry as a priest has been lived out on college campuses where I have met significant numbers of young men and women manifesting what in times past were called "signs of a vocation." Their goodness is unmistakable and their faith, while maturing, is strong. They want to make a difference with their lives and their passion for gospel service literally can't wait. Their spring break, more often than not, is a service trip to Latin America or to struggling areas of the United States or to the Catholic Worker houses in our cities where they work building homes for the poor or tutoring children or serving the needs of the homeless.

The undergraduates among these exceptional young men and women tend to major in the humanities and social sciences with the idea of pursuing careers in the helping professions. The graduate students are drawn to degree programs almost identical to seminary programs of study. A number of these young men and women plan to work in parishes as lay pastoral associates knowing full well they will earn modest wages. Most feel called to ministry *and* called to marriage. They will join a rapidly expanding lay ministry corps that often knows as much or more theology and scripture as their ordained colleagues.

Well educated, highly committed to gospel values, these men and women are the leaders of the church to come. For the most part, they remain untouched by the cultural wars currently gripping the church in North America and Europe. They want to *live* the gospel—which they perceive as the great adventure. And they want to live simply. Most of the men I've spoken to have thought seriously of the priesthood but say they feel an equally strong pull to family life. The women, on the other hand, hardly ever acknowledge any serious thought about religious life.

How many such men and women are there? It is difficult to say but they number more than the students in our seminaries and novitiates. Approximately thirty thousand lay women and men are training to be ecclesial ministers in the United States while the number of graduate seminarians is less than four thousand.

The parents and grandparents of today's college and graduate students, as we have noted earlier, have come of age as adult members of the church. This committed trans-generational segment of the people of God is, for the most part, without illusions. The current crisis, in one stroke, has stripped away much of the Catholic triumphalism of generations past. Aware of the church's faults, wounds, and foibles, they carry on—and provide realistic hope for our future.

Courageous Freedom

In early spring of 2004 Kenneth Untener, the bishop of Saginaw, Michigan, died of a virulent form of leukemia. Widely recognized as one of the more open-minded, pastoral, and prophetic leaders in the U.S. hierarchy, he understood better than most that we really have nothing to fear. His fearlessness betrayed a deep faith and a freedom born of exceptional moral courage. It is well known in Catholic circles that Father Untener's appointment in 1980 as bishop of Saginaw was nearly aborted by a workshop on human sexuality for seminarians that he authorized while rector of the graduate seminary in Detroit. Specifics of the workshop were reported to Rome by some Catholics of the archdiocese who judged them to be inappropriate to the extent of promoting promis cuity. Their complaints put Untener's episcopal appointment in serious jeopardy. Apparently, the intervention of Detroit's Cardinal John Dearden on Untener's behalf persuaded the Vatican to allow his ordination as bishop to proceed.

Robert McClory, writing of Untener's death in the April 9, 2004, issue of the *National Catholic Reporter* provides the source of his remarkable freedom. In the bishop's words:

> Having experienced that right away [the possible cancellation of his appointment as bishop] freed me of the burden of trying to be held in favor. I'm relieved of worrying about what effect something I do will have on my image. Now before I speak out, I only ask, is it true and will it be for the good of the church?

The self-knowledge and personal freedom expressed in these few sentences speak directly to the fear gripping many priests and bishops in the present climate of crisis. In their feudal, clerical culture, being *held in favor* is all important. For what happens in the enclosed world of clericalism is determined more by who is held in favor and who is not held in favor than by objective, external markers of talent, competence, and performance. Priests and bishops with too strong a need to be held in favor (wanting to be held in favor, after all, is human enough) are men who live in fear— fear of displeasing their ecclesial superiors who hold the key to promotions and other signs of ecclesial status. In its extreme form, wanting to be held in favor makes cowards of us all.

Clearly, this seductive pull of the human ego is not restricted to bishops and priests. It is part and parcel of the human condition. It explains why one must *dare* to speak the truth to power and authority. But once this freedom is claimed it bears a great reward—one is relieved of the worry and anxiety that courageous speech or action might have on one's image. Here one's integrity is prized more than one's image or reputation. "Now before I speak out," Bishop Untener said simply, "I only ask, is it true and will it be for the good of the church?" Only a disciple liberated from the concerns of human reputation and grounded in the freedom of the gospel could make such a statement. Untener certainly did not stand alone in modeling courageous freedom, action, and speech. But there were many more of his clerical brothers choosing the safer path than those choosing the path of courageous speech and prophetic leadership.

Extravagant Trust

Angelo Giuseppe Roncalli, the beloved John XXIII, knew how to love. "This was the secret of his personality," said Yves Congar, "he loved people more than power." Out of this love came a remarkable trust. Trust in God, of course, but also trust in his own intuition and trust in the fundamental goodness of the people of God. When he informed his close friend, companion, and secretary Don Loris Capovilla of his intention to call an ecumenical council, John found his plan greeted with strong opposition. Capovilla warned the pope that the council could prove a terrible, embarrassing, exhausting failure. After considering his friend's counsel for a few days, John responded with words that presaged Bishop Untener's release from "the burden of trying to be held in favor." "The trouble is, Don Loris," said the pope, "that you're still not detached enough from self—you're still concerned with having a good reputation. Only when the ego has been trampled underfoot can one be fully and truly free. You are not yet free, Don Loris" (quoted in Thomas Cahill's *Pope John XXIII*).

Freed from the fear of personal failure and its consequences, John was able to trust in God's abiding Spirit. In author Thomas Cahill's words, "John, putting his trust in Providence, was unconcerned about possible failure or even about the stress of a council." In his book *The Journal of a Soul*, Pope John reveals his complete confidence in the maxim: *Absolute trust in God in the present and complete tranquility in regard to what is going to happen in the future.*

Anyone daring to address the current church crisis faces certain criticism and the possibility that he or she may do more harm than good. Still, one may feel compelled to speak. Failure to do so may signal that one is being weighed down by the burden of wanting to be held in favor. Thomas Merton, we observed earlier, put it most succinctly: "In humility is perfect freedom." And in humility and faith is perfect trust. John XXIII understood that it was the Spirit that was ultimately in charge of the church, and that he could trust the Spirit-inspired wisdom of his brother bishops in council.

Without trust in the fundamental goodness of God's people, without trust in the Spirit loose in the world, we compromise our ability to listen to the lessons of our own experience and to listen non-defensively to those who speak out of their love for the church. Without trust we deny the truth we know from our experience of church. Fear, the opposite of trust, prompts us to rely on the present order of things no matter how dysfunctional this order—and the structures supporting it—may be. Fear, we should know by now, leads to attempts at feverish control, to a spirit-killing authoritarianism. Trust, on the other hand, allows the Spirit room to inspire and direct our efforts to renew and reform our church. Such will be the case in times of crisis as well in times of apparent calm. In the epilogue to his book, *John XXIII*, Cahill writes:

> The church is always in need of reformation because it is always in danger of becoming a mere self-protecting institution like all other institutions. When this happens, it follows not the Law of Love but the Law of Institutions, by which it tends to do the opposite of what it professes to do. Just as banks can make people poor, hospitals make them sick, and schools make them ignorant, churches can make them evil—and the history of the papacy is embarrassingly full of examples. More often, however, the papacy has simply taken on the coloration of its time and place: congregational and democratic, oligarchic and imperial, monarchic and absolutist. The hope of John XXIII was to return the church to Pentecost, to a time when the Spirit of God flowed through the congregation, inspiring all. . . .

The dedication in Cahill's *John XXIII* is to Sr. Helen Prejean. He adds, "For the good are always the merry." Pope John's life suggests that it may be equally true that "the trusting are always the merry."

Beyond Resentment

I have never met the English theologian and former Dominican James Alison, but we have exchanged messages through a mutual friend. Alison, a gay Catholic convert, read *The Changing Face of the Priesthood* and offered a gay perspective on my treatment of the destabilizing effect seminaries' gay subculture had on the straight seminarian. Though critical of this aspect of my book, I felt our different voices were nonetheless in harmony. He made this critique in his book *Faith Beyond Resentment: Fragments Catholic and Gay* (Crossroad, 2001). Here Alison chronicles his own journey as a gay, Catholic theologian from resentment and anger to a graced freedom and peace within the church he clearly loves. While I am grateful to Alison for his response to *The Changing Face of the Priesthood*, I am particularly thankful for the liberating wisdom I found in *Faith Beyond Resentment*—a wisdom forged in the resentment and despair of his own personal exile.

His fresh and penetrating reading of the Scriptures and the church's tradition from the perspective of a gay theologian is both challenging and instructive. I mention here but a few of Alison's insights that relate to themes addressed in previous chapters of this book. His is an important voice in the rising chorus.

Hatred. ". . . [H]atred is incapable of being wrong." With these few but striking words, Alison makes clear why it is of critical importance for Catholics in this time of crisis to speak their truth in love. If the faithful, that is, laity *and* clergy, speak from hatred, even resentment, anger, or fear, they will inevitably speak with the arrogance that comes from being certain that one is right—and those who disagree are wrong. When this is the case, the openness of heart essential for genuine listening is foregone. And contemplative conversation emerging from our common ground is rejected as dangerous.

Sacred secrets. Addressing the collapse of the sacred (ecclesial structures and systems) in the case of the prophet Elijah and in the Jewish exile, Alison writes that their secret "is always the victims which it hides, and on whose sacrifice it depends. This then, is what I understand by making space for a heart-close-to-cracking: space where we learn to forge a way of talking about God in the midst of the ruins of the forms of the sacred which are in full collapse." Victim survivors of sexual abuse know well the institutional church's efforts to keep their abuse hidden from the media and public. Faithful Catholics stand in solidarity with abuse victims, their hearts-close-to-cracking, searching for the space to speak and listen as long-standing structures of privilege and control unravel before their eyes.

Integrity. Describing what it is like to be a gay Catholic in the church, Alison observes:

> Typically, our inclusion within the structures of church life comes at a very high price: that of agreeing not to speak honestly, of disguising our experience with a series of euphemisms, of having to maintain, through a coded language shared with other "insiders" within a system, a double life. The message is: you're fine just so long as you don't rock the boat through talking frankly, which is the same as saying: "You're protected while you play the game our way, but the moment that something 'comes to light,' you're out. The moment you say something that causes scandal, watch out!"

Alison describes here a struggle for integrity. Honest speech, whether about homosexuality, clergy sexual abuse and its cover-up, birth control, mandatory celibacy, the role of women, or any of the other neuralgic issues within the church is risky. Better to pretend that everything is basically alright. Yes, there are problems, the faithful are told, but let the institutional church work on them. When people choose silence over honest speech, they take an even more serious risk—the loss of their integrity.

In *Faith Beyond Resentment,* Alison dares to develop a theology of church from his perspective as a gay Catholic theologian. In this critical moment he reminds us that fear and resentment are two of the more powerful forces keeping the church in bondage to structures and systems that no longer work.

A Chorus of Praise

"Prophecy," says Walter Brueggemann, "cannot be separated very long from doxology or it will either wither or become ideology." The voices in the present rising chorus are hardly prophetic in the classical sense of prophecy. They are the voices of Catholic faithful, speaking from their love for the church and out of their experience as adult disciples of Jesus in very trying times. Most of the voices are calling for a more open and inclusive church where the gifts and skills of the people of God are welcomed and developed for the good of the church and the church's mission. Some are the cries of victims abused by clergy and oppressed by church officials who wish they were invisible. A few are the voices of true prophets calling the church to renewal and reform. Each of the various voices in this rising chorus, if they are to be true grace-notes, must sooner than later praise the God in whose name they speak. Otherwise, as Brueggemannn warns, they will wither or succumb to the cultural wars now polarizing the church.

Even though they may be voices weakened by discouragement and criticism, their message will be heard to the extent that it rises up from faith and compassion and leads to praise. As more and more of the laity find their voice, the church as a whole will learn to be wary of voices that do not lead to praise, of voices that condemn and divide. It will learn, too, to be attentive to those whose words not only challenge but heal, to those who speak their truth in love. As Second Isaiah spoke as a prophet of hope for people in exile, he speaks now to people in crisis: "Comfort, give comfort to my people, / says your God. / Speak tenderly to Jerusalem, and proclaim to her / that her service is at an end, / her guilt is expiated" (Isa 40:1-2). Whether the present "exile in place" is about to end or continue for some time into the future, the people of God lift up to God a rising chorus of praise.

Conclusion

This is a moment in the church, we have seen, that requires of its members honest, courageous speech. It is a moment when believers are called to face their anxieties and fears in the silence of contemplative prayer and, with the grace of the Spirit, move beyond and through them into faithful adulthood. It is a time when believers are asked to lay down the burden of being "held in favor." It is a time for the baptized to claim their liberation in the freedom of the Spirit—for the good of the church. What lies ahead is far from clear. What is clear is that we be as true as we can be to this moment in the church's history.

More than ever, in this moment of grace, we need to remember Jesus' response to the Pharisees objecting to the chorus of praise which greeted his triumphal entry into Jerusalem. "If they were to keep silent, I tell you the very stones would cry out" (Luke 19:40).

INDEX